THINGS MOM REALLY, REALLY NEEDS

☐ **SOON**   ☐ **TODAY**   ☐ **RIGHT NOW**   ☐ **FROM NOW ON**

SOON	TODAY	RIGHT NOW	FROM NOW ON
☐ A break	☐ For you to read my mind	☐ Candlelight	☐ Movie night
☐ Less whine	☐ An aspirin	☐ Space	☐ A side of fries
☐ More wine	☐ Some respect	☐ A well-stocked fridge	☐ Some lovin'
☐ Your love	☐ Pizza, toppings my choice	☐ Commiseration	☐ A chauffeur
☐ Chocolate	☐ A good book	☐ To sleep in	☐ Inside voices
☐ A vacation	☐ Work-life balance	☐ A margarita	☐ A little more help
☐ Peace	☐ For you to make dinner	☐ Tantrum absence	☐ Vim
☐ Quiet	☐ A little enthusiasm	☐ The toilet seat down	☐ Vigor
☐ Peace and quiet	☐ To recapture my youth	☐ Someone to take out dog	☐ A good babysitter
☐ A date night	☐ Alone time	☐ Someone to bring in cat	☐ Soft lights
☐ The toilet paper replaced	☐ Alone time in bathroom	☐ A makeover	☐ Soft music
☐ Pampering	☐ Someone to admit I'm right	☐ Costume drama on DVR	☐ Clean clothes
☐ A kiss	☐ A shopping spree	☐ Reality TV on DVR	☐ Time to read
☐ A hug	☐ Attitude of gratitude	☐ Punctuality	☐ A day without dieting
☐ A bear hug	☐ Pie	☐ Endorphin rush	☐ Calm
☐ Someone to listen	☐ A massage	☐ Personal shopper	☐ A friendly phone call
☐ Takeout	☐ An ego massage	☐ Personal schlepper	☐ A day off
☐ A little help	☐ All the answers	☐ A mate to that sock	☐ A smidgen of kindness
☐ To fit into those jeans	☐ Any answer	☐ Time to reflect	☐ A good workout
☐ Privacy	☐ Sweet nothings	☐ A little consideration	☐ A new job
☐ A love note	☐ Personal trainer	☐ Spa day	☐ Even more wine
☐ No complaints	☐ Personal assistant	☐ To be fed grapes	☐ Utter devotion
☐ Hot coffee	☐ A cup of tea	☐ A stiff one	☐ Cupcakes
☐ A hot bath	☐ Therapy	☐ Mother's little helper	☐ Thermostat control
☐ A cold shower	☐ A good night's sleep	☐ A pep talk	☐ A cold drink
☐ Some good gossip	☐ Jewelry	☐ Fewer interruptions	☐ Inner peace
☐ A day in pajamas	☐ To be the center of attention	☐ To win	☐ A day without poop
☐ A day out of sweats	☐ To sit down for a minute	☐ A sugar fix	☐ Sympathy
☐ New shoes	☐ A happy child	☐ Well-behaved inner child	☐ Empathy
☐ A bit of effort	☐ A happy spouse	☐ Well-behaved children	☐ A comfy chair
☐ Barf-free clothing	☐ Praise for my intellect	☐ To get outside	☐ Second helping of dessert
☐ Stress relief	☐ Deodorant	☐ A guilty pleasure	☐ A brisk walk
☐ Family dinner	☐ An apology	☐ A primal scream	☐ A "Please"
☐ Beds all made	☐ Lottery win	☐ A clean kitchen	☐ A "Thank you"
☐ A pick-me-up	☐ A six-pack	☐ More chocolate	☐ A present
☐ Fireman fantasy	☐ Dust bunny eradication	☐ A foot rub	☐ My prince to come
☐ The toothpaste capped	☐ A parking spot	☐ Chores completed	☐ A big bowl of ice cream
☐ A good hair day	☐ No tears	☐ Snuggle time	☐ A serenade
☐ Less laundry	☐ Stain-free day	☐ A good laugh	☐ Grace under pressure
☐ Window-shopping	☐ A haiku	☐ Clean sheets	☐ Mind over matter
☐ Complete obedience	☐ Cuddling	☐ A glass of bubbly	☐ Good will
☐ A chuckle	☐ Coddling	☐ Better neighbors	☐ Flowers
☐ Clean children	☐ A blowout	☐ To hear I'm cool	☐ A miracle
☐ A sincere compliment	☐ An empty dishwasher	☐ To hear I'm hot	☐ Some "me" time
☐ Mani-pedi	☐ You to put on a sweater	☐ Yoga	☐ A good cry
☐ A shoulder to cry on	☐ A nap	☐ Validation	☐ Girl's night out
☐ A random thoughtful act	☐ More help	☐ Breakfast in bed	☐ Romantic dinner
☐ To feel like a million bucks	☐ Complete silence	☐ Control of remote	☐ Full-time help
☐ To look like a million bucks	☐ Extra cheese	☐ A neck rub	☐ Just a little appreciation
☐ A million bucks	☐ A bra that fits	☐ A big smile	☐ Just you

☐ **PLEASE**   ☐ **PRETTY PLEASE**   ☐ **THANK YOU**   ☐ **OR ELSE**

SIGNATURE (ACTUAL NAME OF MOTHER)	MONTH	DAY	YEAR

"IS IT REALLY SO MUCH TO ASK?"

THINGS MOM REALLY, REALLY, REALLY NEEDS

☐ SOON	☐ TODAY	☐ RIGHT NOW	☐ FROM NOW ON
☐ A break	☐ For you to read my mind	☐ Candlelight	☐ Movie night
☐ Less whine	☐ An aspirin	☐ Space	☐ A side of fries
☐ More wine	☐ Some respect	☐ A well-stocked fridge	☐ Some lovin'
☐ Your love	☐ Pizza, toppings my choice	☐ Commiseration	☐ A chauffeur
☐ Chocolate	☐ A good book	☐ To sleep in	☐ Inside voices
☐ A vacation	☐ Work-life balance	☐ A margarita	☐ A little more help
☐ Peace	☐ For you to make dinner	☐ Tantrum absence	☐ Vim
☐ Quiet	☐ A little enthusiasm	☐ The toilet seat down	☐ Vigor
☐ Peace and quiet	☐ To recapture my youth	☐ Someone to take out dog	☐ A good babysitter
☐ A date night	☐ Alone time	☐ Someone to bring in cat	☐ Soft lights
☐ The toilet paper replaced	☐ Alone time in bathroom	☐ A makeover	☐ Soft music
☐ Pampering	☐ Someone to admit I'm right	☐ Costume drama on DVR	☐ Clean clothes
☐ A kiss	☐ A shopping spree	☐ Reality TV on DVR	☐ Time to read
☐ A hug	☐ Attitude of gratitude	☐ Punctuality	☐ A day without dieting
☐ A bear hug	☐ Pie	☐ Endorphin rush	☐ Calm
☐ Someone to listen	☐ A massage	☐ Personal shopper	☐ A friendly phone call
☐ Takeout	☐ An ego massage	☐ Personal schlepper	☐ A day off
☐ A little help	☐ All the answers	☐ A mate to that sock	☐ A smidgen of kindness
☐ To fit into those jeans	☐ Any answer	☐ Time to reflect	☐ A good workout
☐ Privacy	☐ Sweet nothings	☐ A little consideration	☐ A new job
☐ A love note	☐ Personal trainer	☐ Spa day	☐ Even more wine
☐ No complaints	☐ Personal assistant	☐ To be fed grapes	☐ Utter devotion
☐ Hot coffee	☐ A cup of tea	☐ A stiff one	☐ Cupcakes
☐ A hot bath	☐ Therapy	☐ Mother's little helper	☐ Thermostat control
☐ A cold shower	☐ A good night's sleep	☐ A pep talk	☐ A cold drink
☐ Some good gossip	☐ Jewelry	☐ Fewer interruptions	☐ Inner peace
☐ A day in pajamas	☐ To be the center of attention	☐ To win	☐ A day without poop
☐ A day out of sweats	☐ To sit down for a minute	☐ A sugar fix	☐ Sympathy
☐ New shoes	☐ A happy child	☐ Well-behaved inner child	☐ Empathy
☐ A bit of effort	☐ A happy spouse	☐ Well-behaved children	☐ A comfy chair
☐ Barf-free clothing	☐ Praise for my intellect	☐ To get outside	☐ Second helping of dessert
☐ Stress relief	☐ Deodorant	☐ A guilty pleasure	☐ A brisk walk
☐ Family dinner	☐ An apology	☐ A primal scream	☐ A "Please"
☐ Beds all made	☐ Lottery win	☐ A clean kitchen	☐ A "Thank you"
☐ A pick-me-up	☐ A six-pack	☐ More chocolate	☐ A present
☐ Fireman fantasy	☐ Dust bunny eradication	☐ A foot rub	☐ My prince to come
☐ The toothpaste capped	☐ A parking spot	☐ Chores completed	☐ A big bowl of ice cream
☐ A good hair day	☐ No tears	☐ Snuggle time	☐ A serenade
☐ Less laundry	☐ Stain-free day	☐ A good laugh	☐ Grace under pressure
☐ Window-shopping	☐ A haiku	☐ Clean sheets	☐ Mind over matter
☐ Complete obedience	☐ Cuddling	☐ A glass of bubbly	☐ Good will
☐ A chuckle	☐ Coddling	☐ Better neighbors	☐ Flowers
☐ Clean children	☐ A blowout	☐ To hear I'm cool	☐ A miracle
☐ A sincere compliment	☐ An empty dishwasher	☐ To hear I'm hot	☐ Some "me" time
☐ Mani-pedi	☐ You to put on a sweater	☐ Yoga	☐ A good cry
☐ A shoulder to cry on	☐ A nap	☐ Validation	☐ Girl's night out
☐ A random thoughtful act	☐ More help	☐ Breakfast in bed	☐ Romantic dinner
☐ To feel like a million bucks	☐ Complete silence	☐ Control of remote	☐ Full-time help
☐ To look like a million bucks	☐ Extra cheese	☐ A neck rub	☐ Just a little appreciation
☐ A million bucks	☐ A bra that fits	☐ A big smile	☐ Just you

☐ PLEASE	☐ PRETTY PLEASE	☐ THANK YOU	☐ OR ELSE

SIGNATURE (ACTUAL NAME OF MOTHER)		MONTH : DAY : YEAR

"IS IT REALLY SO MUCH TO ASK?"

THINGS MOM REALLY, REALLY, REALLY NEEDS

☐ SOON	☐ TODAY	☐ RIGHT NOW	☐ FROM NOW ON
☐ A break	☐ For you to read my mind	☐ Candlelight	☐ Movie night
☐ Less whine	☐ An aspirin	☐ Space	☐ A side of fries
☐ More wine	☐ Some respect	☐ A well-stocked fridge	☐ Some lovin'
☐ Your love	☐ Pizza, toppings my choice	☐ Commiseration	☐ A chauffeur
☐ Chocolate	☐ A good book	☐ To sleep in	☐ Inside voices
☐ A vacation	☐ Work-life balance	☐ A margarita	☐ A little more help
☐ Peace	☐ For you to make dinner	☐ Tantrum absence	☐ Vim
☐ Quiet	☐ A little enthusiasm	☐ The toilet seat down	☐ Vigor
☐ Peace and quiet	☐ To recapture my youth	☐ Someone to take out dog	☐ A good babysitter
☐ A date night	☐ Alone time	☐ Someone to bring in cat	☐ Soft lights
☐ The toilet paper replaced	☐ Alone time in bathroom	☐ A makeover	☐ Soft music
☐ Pampering	☐ Someone to admit I'm right	☐ Costume drama on DVR	☐ Clean clothes
☐ A kiss	☐ A shopping spree	☐ Reality TV on DVR	☐ Time to read
☐ A hug	☐ Attitude of gratitude	☐ Punctuality	☐ A day without dieting
☐ A bear hug	☐ Pie	☐ Endorphin rush	☐ Calm
☐ Someone to listen	☐ A massage	☐ Personal shopper	☐ A friendly phone call
☐ Takeout	☐ An ego massage	☐ Personal schlepper	☐ A day off
☐ A little help	☐ All the answers	☐ A mate to that sock	☐ A smidgen of kindness
☐ To fit into those jeans	☐ Any answer	☐ Time to reflect	☐ A good workout
☐ Privacy	☐ Sweet nothings	☐ A little consideration	☐ A new job
☐ A love note	☐ Personal trainer	☐ Spa day	☐ Even more wine
☐ No complaints	☐ Personal assistant	☐ To be fed grapes	☐ Utter devotion
☐ Hot coffee	☐ A cup of tea	☐ A stiff one	☐ Cupcakes
☐ A hot bath	☐ Therapy	☐ Mother's little helper	☐ Thermostat control
☐ A cold shower	☐ A good night's sleep	☐ A pep talk	☐ A cold drink
☐ Some good gossip	☐ Jewelry	☐ Fewer interruptions	☐ Inner peace
☐ A day in pajamas	☐ To be the center of attention	☐ To win	☐ A day without poop
☐ A day out of sweats	☐ To sit down for a minute	☐ A sugar fix	☐ Sympathy
☐ New shoes	☐ A happy child	☐ Well-behaved inner child	☐ Empathy
☐ A bit of effort	☐ A happy spouse	☐ Well-behaved children	☐ A comfy chair
☐ Barf-free clothing	☐ Praise for my intellect	☐ To get outside	☐ Second helping of dessert
☐ Stress relief	☐ Deodorant	☐ A guilty pleasure	☐ A brisk walk
☐ Family dinner	☐ An apology	☐ A primal scream	☐ A "Please"
☐ Beds all made	☐ Lottery win	☐ A clean kitchen	☐ A "Thank you"
☐ A pick-me-up	☐ A six-pack	☐ More chocolate	☐ A present
☐ Fireman fantasy	☐ Dust bunny eradication	☐ A foot rub	☐ My prince to come
☐ The toothpaste capped	☐ A parking spot	☐ Chores completed	☐ A big bowl of ice cream
☐ A good hair day	☐ No tears	☐ Snuggle time	☐ A serenade
☐ Less laundry	☐ Stain-free day	☐ A good laugh	☐ Grace under pressure
☐ Window-shopping	☐ A haiku	☐ Clean sheets	☐ Mind over matter
☐ Complete obedience	☐ Cuddling	☐ A glass of bubbly	☐ Good will
☐ A chuckle	☐ Coddling	☐ Better neighbors	☐ Flowers
☐ Clean children	☐ A blowout	☐ To hear I'm cool	☐ A miracle
☐ A sincere compliment	☐ An empty dishwasher	☐ To hear I'm hot	☐ Some "me" time
☐ Mani-pedi	☐ You to put on a sweater	☐ Yoga	☐ A good cry
☐ A shoulder to cry on	☐ A nap	☐ Validation	☐ Girl's night out
☐ A random thoughtful act	☐ More help	☐ Breakfast in bed	☐ Romantic dinner
☐ To feel like a million bucks	☐ Complete silence	☐ Control of remote	☐ Full-time help
☐ To look like a million bucks	☐ Extra cheese	☐ A neck rub	☐ Just a little appreciation
☐ A million bucks	☐ A bra that fits	☐ A big smile	☐ Just you

☐ PLEASE	☐ PRETTY PLEASE	☐ THANK YOU	☐ OR ELSE

SIGNATURE (ACTUAL NAME OF MOTHER) | MONTH | DAY | YEAR

"IS IT REALLY SO MUCH TO ASK?"

THINGS MOM REALLY, REALLY, REALLY NEEDS

☐ **SOON**   ☐ **TODAY**   ☐ **RIGHT NOW**   ☐ **FROM NOW ON**

SOON	TODAY	RIGHT NOW	FROM NOW ON
☐ A break	☐ For you to read my mind	☐ Candlelight	☐ Movie night
☐ Less whine	☐ An aspirin	☐ Space	☐ A side of fries
☐ More wine	☐ Some respect	☐ A well-stocked fridge	☐ Some lovin'
☐ Your love	☐ Pizza, toppings my choice	☐ Commiseration	☐ A chauffeur
☐ Chocolate	☐ A good book	☐ To sleep in	☐ Inside voices
☐ A vacation	☐ Work-life balance	☐ A margarita	☐ A little more help
☐ Peace	☐ For you to make dinner	☐ Tantrum absence	☐ Vim
☐ Quiet	☐ A little enthusiasm	☐ The toilet seat down	☐ Vigor
☐ Peace and quiet	☐ To recapture my youth	☐ Someone to take out dog	☐ A good babysitter
☐ A date night	☐ Alone time	☐ Someone to bring in cat	☐ Soft lights
☐ The toilet paper replaced	☐ Alone time in bathroom	☐ A makeover	☐ Soft music
☐ Pampering	☐ Someone to admit I'm right	☐ Costume drama on DVR	☐ Clean clothes
☐ A kiss	☐ A shopping spree	☐ Reality TV on DVR	☐ Time to read
☐ A hug	☐ Attitude of gratitude	☐ Punctuality	☐ A day without dieting
☐ A bear hug	☐ Pie	☐ Endorphin rush	☐ Calm
☐ Someone to listen	☐ A massage	☐ Personal shopper	☐ A friendly phone call
☐ Takeout	☐ An ego massage	☐ Personal schlepper	☐ A day off
☐ A little help	☐ All the answers	☐ A mate to that sock	☐ A smidgen of kindness
☐ To fit into those jeans	☐ Any answer	☐ Time to reflect	☐ A good workout
☐ Privacy	☐ Sweet nothings	☐ A little consideration	☐ A new job
☐ A love note	☐ Personal trainer	☐ Spa day	☐ Even more wine
☐ No complaints	☐ Personal assistant	☐ To be fed grapes	☐ Utter devotion
☐ Hot coffee	☐ A cup of tea	☐ A stiff one	☐ Cupcakes
☐ A hot bath	☐ Therapy	☐ Mother's little helper	☐ Thermostat control
☐ A cold shower	☐ A good night's sleep	☐ A pep talk	☐ A cold drink
☐ Some good gossip	☐ Jewelry	☐ Fewer interruptions	☐ Inner peace
☐ A day in pajamas	☐ To be the center of attention	☐ To win	☐ A day without poop
☐ A day out of sweats	☐ To sit down for a minute	☐ A sugar fix	☐ Sympathy
☐ New shoes	☐ A happy child	☐ Well-behaved inner child	☐ Empathy
☐ A bit of effort	☐ A happy spouse	☐ Well-behaved children	☐ A comfy chair
☐ Barf-free clothing	☐ Praise for my intellect	☐ To get outside	☐ Second helping of dessert
☐ Stress relief	☐ Deodorant	☐ A guilty pleasure	☐ A brisk walk
☐ Family dinner	☐ An apology	☐ A primal scream	☐ A "Please"
☐ Beds all made	☐ Lottery win	☐ A clean kitchen	☐ A "Thank you"
☐ A pick-me-up	☐ A six-pack	☐ More chocolate	☐ A present
☐ Fireman fantasy	☐ Dust bunny eradication	☐ A foot rub	☐ My prince to come
☐ The toothpaste capped	☐ A parking spot	☐ Chores completed	☐ A big bowl of ice cream
☐ A good hair day	☐ No tears	☐ Snuggle time	☐ A serenade
☐ Less laundry	☐ Stain-free day	☐ A good laugh	☐ Grace under pressure
☐ Window-shopping	☐ A haiku	☐ Clean sheets	☐ Mind over matter
☐ Complete obedience	☐ Cuddling	☐ A glass of bubbly	☐ Good will
☐ A chuckle	☐ Coddling	☐ Better neighbors	☐ Flowers
☐ Clean children	☐ A blowout	☐ To hear I'm cool	☐ A miracle
☐ A sincere compliment	☐ An empty dishwasher	☐ To hear I'm hot	☐ Some "me" time
☐ Mani-pedi	☐ You to put on a sweater	☐ Yoga	☐ A good cry
☐ A shoulder to cry on	☐ A nap	☐ Validation	☐ Girl's night out
☐ A random thoughtful act	☐ More help	☐ Breakfast in bed	☐ Romantic dinner
☐ To feel like a million bucks	☐ Complete silence	☐ Control of remote	☐ Full-time help
☐ To look like a million bucks	☐ Extra cheese	☐ A neck rub	☐ Just a little appreciation
☐ A million bucks	☐ A bra that fits	☐ A big smile	☐ Just you

☐ **PLEASE**   ☐ **PRETTY PLEASE**   ☐ **THANK YOU**   ☐ **OR ELSE**

SIGNATURE (ACTUAL NAME OF MOTHER)

| MONTH | DAY | YEAR |

"IS IT REALLY SO MUCH TO ASK?"

THINGS MOM REALLY, REALLY, REALLY NEEDS

☐ **SOON** ☐ **TODAY** ☐ **RIGHT NOW** ☐ **FROM NOW ON**

☐ A break	☐ For you to read my mind	☐ Candlelight	☐ Movie night
☐ Less whine	☐ An aspirin	☐ Space	☐ A side of fries
☐ More wine	☐ Some respect	☐ A well-stocked fridge	☐ Some lovin'
☐ Your love	☐ Pizza, toppings my choice	☐ Commiseration	☐ A chauffeur
☐ Chocolate	☐ A good book	☐ To sleep in	☐ Inside voices
☐ A vacation	☐ Work-life balance	☐ A margarita	☐ A little more help
☐ Peace	☐ For you to make dinner	☐ Tantrum absence	☐ Vim
☐ Quiet	☐ A little enthusiasm	☐ The toilet seat down	☐ Vigor
☐ Peace and quiet	☐ To recapture my youth	☐ Someone to take out dog	☐ A good babysitter
☐ A date night	☐ Alone time	☐ Someone to bring in cat	☐ Soft lights
☐ The toilet paper replaced	☐ Alone time in bathroom	☐ A makeover	☐ Soft music
☐ Pampering	☐ Someone to admit I'm right	☐ Costume drama on DVR	☐ Clean clothes
☐ A kiss	☐ A shopping spree	☐ Reality TV on DVR	☐ Time to read
☐ A hug	☐ Attitude of gratitude	☐ Punctuality	☐ A day without dieting
☐ A bear hug	☐ Pie	☐ Endorphin rush	☐ Calm
☐ Someone to listen	☐ A massage	☐ Personal shopper	☐ A friendly phone call
☐ Takeout	☐ An ego massage	☐ Personal schlepper	☐ A day off
☐ A little help	☐ All the answers	☐ A mate to that sock	☐ A smidgen of kindness
☐ To fit into those jeans	☐ Any answer	☐ Time to reflect	☐ A good workout
☐ Privacy	☐ Sweet nothings	☐ A little consideration	☐ A new job
☐ A love note	☐ Personal trainer	☐ Spa day	☐ Even more wine
☐ No complaints	☐ Personal assistant	☐ To be fed grapes	☐ Utter devotion
☐ Hot coffee	☐ A cup of tea	☐ A stiff one	☐ Cupcakes
☐ A hot bath	☐ Therapy	☐ Mother's little helper	☐ Thermostat control
☐ A cold shower	☐ A good night's sleep	☐ A pep talk	☐ A cold drink
☐ Some good gossip	☐ Jewelry	☐ Fewer interruptions	☐ Inner peace
☐ A day in pajamas	☐ To be the center of attention	☐ To win	☐ A day without poop
☐ A day out of sweats	☐ To sit down for a minute	☐ A sugar fix	☐ Sympathy
☐ New shoes	☐ A happy child	☐ Well-behaved inner child	☐ Empathy
☐ A bit of effort	☐ A happy spouse	☐ Well-behaved children	☐ A comfy chair
☐ Barf-free clothing	☐ Praise for my intellect	☐ To get outside	☐ Second helping of dessert
☐ Stress relief	☐ Deodorant	☐ A guilty pleasure	☐ A brisk walk
☐ Family dinner	☐ An apology	☐ A primal scream	☐ A "Please"
☐ Beds all made	☐ Lottery win	☐ A clean kitchen	☐ A "Thank you"
☐ A pick-me-up	☐ A six-pack	☐ More chocolate	☐ A present
☐ Fireman fantasy	☐ Dust bunny eradication	☐ A foot rub	☐ My prince to come
☐ The toothpaste capped	☐ A parking spot	☐ Chores completed	☐ A big bowl of ice cream
☐ A good hair day	☐ No tears	☐ Snuggle time	☐ A serenade
☐ Less laundry	☐ Stain-free day	☐ A good laugh	☐ Grace under pressure
☐ Window-shopping	☐ A haiku	☐ Clean sheets	☐ Mind over matter
☐ Complete obedience	☐ Cuddling	☐ A glass of bubbly	☐ Good will
☐ A chuckle	☐ Coddling	☐ Better neighbors	☐ Flowers
☐ Clean children	☐ A blowout	☐ To hear I'm cool	☐ A miracle
☐ A sincere compliment	☐ An empty dishwasher	☐ To hear I'm hot	☐ Some "me" time
☐ Mani-pedi	☐ You to put on a sweater	☐ Yoga	☐ A good cry
☐ A shoulder to cry on	☐ A nap	☐ Validation	☐ Girl's night out
☐ A random thoughtful act	☐ More help	☐ Breakfast in bed	☐ Romantic dinner
☐ To feel like a million bucks	☐ Complete silence	☐ Control of remote	☐ Full-time help
☐ To look like a million bucks	☐ Extra cheese	☐ A neck rub	☐ Just a little appreciation
☐ A million bucks	☐ A bra that fits	☐ A big smile	☐ Just you

☐ **PLEASE** ☐ **PRETTY PLEASE** ☐ **THANK YOU** ☐ **OR ELSE**

SIGNATURE (ACTUAL NAME OF MOTHER)

MONTH · DAY · YEAR

"IS IT REALLY SO MUCH TO ASK?"

KNOCKKNOCKSTUFF.COM ▪ © 2014 WHO'S THERE INC.

THINGS MOM REALLY, REALLY, REALLY NEEDS

☐ **SOON**   ☐ **TODAY**   ☐ **RIGHT NOW**   ☐ **FROM NOW ON**

SOON	TODAY	RIGHT NOW	FROM NOW ON
☐ A break	☐ For you to read my mind	☐ Candlelight	☐ Movie night
☐ Less whine	☐ An aspirin	☐ Space	☐ A side of fries
☐ More wine	☐ Some respect	☐ A well-stocked fridge	☐ Some lovin'
☐ Your love	☐ Pizza, toppings my choice	☐ Commiseration	☐ A chauffeur
☐ Chocolate	☐ A good book	☐ To sleep in	☐ Inside voices
☐ A vacation	☐ Work-life balance	☐ A margarita	☐ A little more help
☐ Peace	☐ For you to make dinner	☐ Tantrum absence	☐ Vim
☐ Quiet	☐ A little enthusiasm	☐ The toilet seat down	☐ Vigor
☐ Peace and quiet	☐ To recapture my youth	☐ Someone to take out dog	☐ A good babysitter
☐ A date night	☐ Alone time	☐ Someone to bring in cat	☐ Soft lights
☐ The toilet paper replaced	☐ Alone time in bathroom	☐ A makeover	☐ Soft music
☐ Pampering	☐ Someone to admit I'm right	☐ Costume drama on DVR	☐ Clean clothes
☐ A kiss	☐ A shopping spree	☐ Reality TV on DVR	☐ Time to read
☐ A hug	☐ Attitude of gratitude	☐ Punctuality	☐ A day without dieting
☐ A bear hug	☐ Pie	☐ Endorphin rush	☐ Calm
☐ Someone to listen	☐ A massage	☐ Personal shopper	☐ A friendly phone call
☐ Takeout	☐ An ego massage	☐ Personal schlepper	☐ A day off
☐ A little help	☐ All the answers	☐ A mate to that sock	☐ A smidgen of kindness
☐ To fit into those jeans	☐ Any answer	☐ Time to reflect	☐ A good workout
☐ Privacy	☐ Sweet nothings	☐ A little consideration	☐ A new job
☐ A love note	☐ Personal trainer	☐ Spa day	☐ Even more wine
☐ No complaints	☐ Personal assistant	☐ To be fed grapes	☐ Utter devotion
☐ Hot coffee	☐ A cup of tea	☐ A stiff one	☐ Cupcakes
☐ A hot bath	☐ Therapy	☐ Mother's little helper	☐ Thermostat control
☐ A cold shower	☐ A good night's sleep	☐ A pep talk	☐ A cold drink
☐ Some good gossip	☐ Jewelry	☐ Fewer interruptions	☐ Inner peace
☐ A day in pajamas	☐ To be the center of attention	☐ To win	☐ A day without poop
☐ A day out of sweats	☐ To sit down for a minute	☐ A sugar fix	☐ Sympathy
☐ New shoes	☐ A happy child	☐ Well-behaved inner child	☐ Empathy
☐ A bit of effort	☐ A happy spouse	☐ Well-behaved children	☐ A comfy chair
☐ Barf-free clothing	☐ Praise for my intellect	☐ To get outside	☐ Second helping of dessert
☐ Stress relief	☐ Deodorant	☐ A guilty pleasure	☐ A brisk walk
☐ Family dinner	☐ An apology	☐ A primal scream	☐ A "Please"
☐ Beds all made	☐ Lottery win	☐ A clean kitchen	☐ A "Thank you"
☐ A pick-me-up	☐ A six-pack	☐ More chocolate	☐ A present
☐ Fireman fantasy	☐ Dust bunny eradication	☐ A foot rub	☐ My prince to come
☐ The toothpaste capped	☐ A parking spot	☐ Chores completed	☐ A big bowl of ice cream
☐ A good hair day	☐ No tears	☐ Snuggle time	☐ A serenade
☐ Less laundry	☐ Stain-free day	☐ A good laugh	☐ Grace under pressure
☐ Window-shopping	☐ A haiku	☐ Clean sheets	☐ Mind over matter
☐ Complete obedience	☐ Cuddling	☐ A glass of bubbly	☐ Good will
☐ A chuckle	☐ Coddling	☐ Better neighbors	☐ Flowers
☐ Clean children	☐ A blowout	☐ To hear I'm cool	☐ A miracle
☐ A sincere compliment	☐ An empty dishwasher	☐ To hear I'm hot	☐ Some "me" time
☐ Mani-pedi	☐ You to put on a sweater	☐ Yoga	☐ A good cry
☐ A shoulder to cry on	☐ A nap	☐ Validation	☐ Girl's night out
☐ A random thoughtful act	☐ More help	☐ Breakfast in bed	☐ Romantic dinner
☐ To feel like a million bucks	☐ Complete silence	☐ Control of remote	☐ Full-time help
☐ To look like a million bucks	☐ Extra cheese	☐ A neck rub	☐ Just a little appreciation
☐ A million bucks	☐ A bra that fits	☐ A big smile	☐ Just you

☐ **PLEASE**   ☐ **PRETTY PLEASE**   ☐ **THANK YOU**   ☐ **OR ELSE**

SIGNATURE (ACTUAL NAME OF MOTHER)   MONTH   DAY   YEAR

"IS IT REALLY SO MUCH TO ASK?"

KNOCKKNOCKSTUFF.COM ■ © 2014 WHO'S THERE INC.

THINGS MOM REALLY, REALLY, REALLY NEEDS

☐ **SOON**   ☐ **TODAY**   ☐ **RIGHT NOW**   ☐ **FROM NOW ON**

SOON	TODAY	RIGHT NOW	FROM NOW ON
☐ A break	☐ For you to read my mind	☐ Candlelight	☐ Movie night
☐ Less whine	☐ An aspirin	☐ Space	☐ A side of fries
☐ More wine	☐ Some respect	☐ A well-stocked fridge	☐ Some lovin'
☐ Your love	☐ Pizza, toppings my choice	☐ Commiseration	☐ A chauffeur
☐ Chocolate	☐ A good book	☐ To sleep in	☐ Inside voices
☐ A vacation	☐ Work-life balance	☐ A margarita	☐ A little more help
☐ Peace	☐ For you to make dinner	☐ Tantrum absence	☐ Vim
☐ Quiet	☐ A little enthusiasm	☐ The toilet seat down	☐ Vigor
☐ Peace and quiet	☐ To recapture my youth	☐ Someone to take out dog	☐ A good babysitter
☐ A date night	☐ Alone time	☐ Someone to bring in cat	☐ Soft lights
☐ The toilet paper replaced	☐ Alone time in bathroom	☐ A makeover	☐ Soft music
☐ Pampering	☐ Someone to admit I'm right	☐ Costume drama on DVR	☐ Clean clothes
☐ A kiss	☐ A shopping spree	☐ Reality TV on DVR	☐ Time to read
☐ A hug	☐ Attitude of gratitude	☐ Punctuality	☐ A day without dieting
☐ A bear hug	☐ Pie	☐ Endorphin rush	☐ Calm
☐ Someone to listen	☐ A massage	☐ Personal shopper	☐ A friendly phone call
☐ Takeout	☐ An ego massage	☐ Personal schlepper	☐ A day off
☐ A little help	☐ All the answers	☐ A mate to that sock	☐ A smidgen of kindness
☐ To fit into those jeans	☐ Any answer	☐ Time to reflect	☐ A good workout
☐ Privacy	☐ Sweet nothings	☐ A little consideration	☐ A new job
☐ A love note	☐ Personal trainer	☐ Spa day	☐ Even more wine
☐ No complaints	☐ Personal assistant	☐ To be fed grapes	☐ Utter devotion
☐ Hot coffee	☐ A cup of tea	☐ A stiff one	☐ Cupcakes
☐ A hot bath	☐ Therapy	☐ Mother's little helper	☐ Thermostat control
☐ A cold shower	☐ A good night's sleep	☐ A pep talk	☐ A cold drink
☐ Some good gossip	☐ Jewelry	☐ Fewer interruptions	☐ Inner peace
☐ A day in pajamas	☐ To be the center of attention	☐ To win	☐ A day without poop
☐ A day out of sweats	☐ To sit down for a minute	☐ A sugar fix	☐ Sympathy
☐ New shoes	☐ A happy child	☐ Well-behaved inner child	☐ Empathy
☐ A bit of effort	☐ A happy spouse	☐ Well-behaved children	☐ A comfy chair
☐ Barf-free clothing	☐ Praise for my intellect	☐ To get outside	☐ Second helping of dessert
☐ Stress relief	☐ Deodorant	☐ A guilty pleasure	☐ A brisk walk
☐ Family dinner	☐ An apology	☐ A primal scream	☐ A "Please"
☐ Beds all made	☐ Lottery win	☐ A clean kitchen	☐ A "Thank you"
☐ A pick-me-up	☐ A six-pack	☐ More chocolate	☐ A present
☐ Fireman fantasy	☐ Dust bunny eradication	☐ A foot rub	☐ My prince to come
☐ The toothpaste capped	☐ A parking spot	☐ Chores completed	☐ A big bowl of ice cream
☐ A good hair day	☐ No tears	☐ Snuggle time	☐ A serenade
☐ Less laundry	☐ Stain-free day	☐ A good laugh	☐ Grace under pressure
☐ Window-shopping	☐ A haiku	☐ Clean sheets	☐ Mind over matter
☐ Complete obedience	☐ Cuddling	☐ A glass of bubbly	☐ Good will
☐ A chuckle	☐ Coddling	☐ Better neighbors	☐ Flowers
☐ Clean children	☐ A blowout	☐ To hear I'm cool	☐ A miracle
☐ A sincere compliment	☐ An empty dishwasher	☐ To hear I'm hot	☐ Some "me" time
☐ Mani-pedi	☐ You to put on a sweater	☐ Yoga	☐ A good cry
☐ A shoulder to cry on	☐ A nap	☐ Validation	☐ Girl's night out
☐ A random thoughtful act	☐ More help	☐ Breakfast in bed	☐ Romantic dinner
☐ To feel like a million bucks	☐ Complete silence	☐ Control of remote	☐ Full-time help
☐ To look like a million bucks	☐ Extra cheese	☐ A neck rub	☐ Just a little appreciation
☐ A million bucks	☐ A bra that fits	☐ A big smile	☐ Just you

☐ **PLEASE**   ☐ **PRETTY PLEASE**   ☐ **THANK YOU**   ☐ **OR ELSE**

SIGNATURE (ACTUAL NAME OF MOTHER)

| MONTH | DAY | YEAR |

"IS IT REALLY SO MUCH TO ASK?"

THINGS MOM REALLY, REALLY, REALLY NEEDS

☐ **SOON**   ☐ **TODAY**   ☐ **RIGHT NOW**   ☐ **FROM NOW ON**

☐ A break	☐ For you to read my mind	☐ Candlelight	☐ Movie night
☐ Less whine	☐ An aspirin	☐ Space	☐ A side of fries
☐ More wine	☐ Some respect	☐ A well-stocked fridge	☐ Some lovin'
☐ Your love	☐ Pizza, toppings my choice	☐ Commiseration	☐ A chauffeur
☐ Chocolate	☐ A good book	☐ To sleep in	☐ Inside voices
☐ A vacation	☐ Work-life balance	☐ A margarita	☐ A little more help
☐ Peace	☐ For you to make dinner	☐ Tantrum absence	☐ Vim
☐ Quiet	☐ A little enthusiasm	☐ The toilet seat down	☐ Vigor
☐ Peace and quiet	☐ To recapture my youth	☐ Someone to take out dog	☐ A good babysitter
☐ A date night	☐ Alone time	☐ Someone to bring in cat	☐ Soft lights
☐ The toilet paper replaced	☐ Alone time in bathroom	☐ A makeover	☐ Soft music
☐ Pampering	☐ Someone to admit I'm right	☐ Costume drama on DVR	☐ Clean clothes
☐ A kiss	☐ A shopping spree	☐ Reality TV on DVR	☐ Time to read
☐ A hug	☐ Attitude of gratitude	☐ Punctuality	☐ A day without dieting
☐ A bear hug	☐ Pie	☐ Endorphin rush	☐ Calm
☐ Someone to listen	☐ A massage	☐ Personal shopper	☐ A friendly phone call
☐ Takeout	☐ An ego massage	☐ Personal schlepper	☐ A day off
☐ A little help	☐ All the answers	☐ A mate to that sock	☐ A smidgen of kindness
☐ To fit into those jeans	☐ Any answer	☐ Time to reflect	☐ A good workout
☐ Privacy	☐ Sweet nothings	☐ A little consideration	☐ A new job
☐ A love note	☐ Personal trainer	☐ Spa day	☐ Even more wine
☐ No complaints	☐ Personal assistant	☐ To be fed grapes	☐ Utter devotion
☐ Hot coffee	☐ A cup of tea	☐ A stiff one	☐ Cupcakes
☐ A hot bath	☐ Therapy	☐ Mother's little helper	☐ Thermostat control
☐ A cold shower	☐ A good night's sleep	☐ A pep talk	☐ A cold drink
☐ Some good gossip	☐ Jewelry	☐ Fewer interruptions	☐ Inner peace
☐ A day in pajamas	☐ To be the center of attention	☐ To win	☐ A day without poop
☐ A day out of sweats	☐ To sit down for a minute	☐ A sugar fix	☐ Sympathy
☐ New shoes	☐ A happy child	☐ Well-behaved inner child	☐ Empathy
☐ A bit of effort	☐ A happy spouse	☐ Well-behaved children	☐ A comfy chair
☐ Barf-free clothing	☐ Praise for my intellect	☐ To get outside	☐ Second helping of dessert
☐ Stress relief	☐ Deodorant	☐ A guilty pleasure	☐ A brisk walk
☐ Family dinner	☐ An apology	☐ A primal scream	☐ A "Please"
☐ Beds all made	☐ Lottery win	☐ A clean kitchen	☐ A "Thank you"
☐ A pick-me-up	☐ A six-pack	☐ More chocolate	☐ A present
☐ Fireman fantasy	☐ Dust bunny eradication	☐ A foot rub	☐ My prince to come
☐ The toothpaste capped	☐ A parking spot	☐ Chores completed	☐ A big bowl of ice cream
☐ A good hair day	☐ No tears	☐ Snuggle time	☐ A serenade
☐ Less laundry	☐ Stain-free day	☐ A good laugh	☐ Grace under pressure
☐ Window-shopping	☐ A haiku	☐ Clean sheets	☐ Mind over matter
☐ Complete obedience	☐ Cuddling	☐ A glass of bubbly	☐ Good will
☐ A chuckle	☐ Coddling	☐ Better neighbors	☐ Flowers
☐ Clean children	☐ A blowout	☐ To hear I'm cool	☐ A miracle
☐ A sincere compliment	☐ An empty dishwasher	☐ To hear I'm hot	☐ Some "me" time
☐ Mani-pedi	☐ You to put on a sweater	☐ Yoga	☐ A good cry
☐ A shoulder to cry on	☐ A nap	☐ Validation	☐ Girl's night out
☐ A random thoughtful act	☐ More help	☐ Breakfast in bed	☐ Romantic dinner
☐ To feel like a million bucks	☐ Complete silence	☐ Control of remote	☐ Full-time help
☐ To look like a million bucks	☐ Extra cheese	☐ A neck rub	☐ Just a little appreciation
☐ A million bucks	☐ A bra that fits	☐ A big smile	☐ Just you

☐ **PLEASE**   ☐ **PRETTY PLEASE**   ☐ **THANK YOU**   ☐ **OR ELSE**

SIGNATURE (ACTUAL NAME OF MOTHER) | MONTH | DAY | YEAR

"IS IT REALLY SO MUCH TO ASK?"

KNOCKKNOCKSTUFF.COM ▪ © 2014 WHO'S THERE INC.

THINGS MOM REALLY, REALLY, REALLY NEEDS

☐ **SOON**　　☐ **TODAY**　　☐ **RIGHT NOW**　　☐ **FROM NOW ON**

☐ A break	☐ For you to read my mind	☐ Candlelight	☐ Movie night
☐ Less whine	☐ An aspirin	☐ Space	☐ A side of fries
☐ More wine	☐ Some respect	☐ A well-stocked fridge	☐ Some lovin'
☐ Your love	☐ Pizza, toppings my choice	☐ Commiseration	☐ A chauffeur
☐ Chocolate	☐ A good book	☐ To sleep in	☐ Inside voices
☐ A vacation	☐ Work-life balance	☐ A margarita	☐ A little more help
☐ Peace	☐ For you to make dinner	☐ Tantrum absence	☐ Vim
☐ Quiet	☐ A little enthusiasm	☐ The toilet seat down	☐ Vigor
☐ Peace and quiet	☐ To recapture my youth	☐ Someone to take out dog	☐ A good babysitter
☐ A date night	☐ Alone time	☐ Someone to bring in cat	☐ Soft lights
☐ The toilet paper replaced	☐ Alone time in bathroom	☐ A makeover	☐ Soft music
☐ Pampering	☐ Someone to admit I'm right	☐ Costume drama on DVR	☐ Clean clothes
☐ A kiss	☐ A shopping spree	☐ Reality TV on DVR	☐ Time to read
☐ A hug	☐ Attitude of gratitude	☐ Punctuality	☐ A day without dieting
☐ A bear hug	☐ Pie	☐ Endorphin rush	☐ Calm
☐ Someone to listen	☐ A massage	☐ Personal shopper	☐ A friendly phone call
☐ Takeout	☐ An ego massage	☐ Personal schlepper	☐ A day off
☐ A little help	☐ All the answers	☐ A mate to that sock	☐ A smidgen of kindness
☐ To fit into those jeans	☐ Any answer	☐ Time to reflect	☐ A good workout
☐ Privacy	☐ Sweet nothings	☐ A little consideration	☐ A new job
☐ A love note	☐ Personal trainer	☐ Spa day	☐ Even more wine
☐ No complaints	☐ Personal assistant	☐ To be fed grapes	☐ Utter devotion
☐ Hot coffee	☐ A cup of tea	☐ A stiff one	☐ Cupcakes
☐ A hot bath	☐ Therapy	☐ Mother's little helper	☐ Thermostat control
☐ A cold shower	☐ A good night's sleep	☐ A pep talk	☐ A cold drink
☐ Some good gossip	☐ Jewelry	☐ Fewer interruptions	☐ Inner peace
☐ A day in pajamas	☐ To be the center of attention	☐ To win	☐ A day without poop
☐ A day out of sweats	☐ To sit down for a minute	☐ A sugar fix	☐ Sympathy
☐ New shoes	☐ A happy child	☐ Well-behaved inner child	☐ Empathy
☐ A bit of effort	☐ A happy spouse	☐ Well-behaved children	☐ A comfy chair
☐ Barf-free clothing	☐ Praise for my intellect	☐ To get outside	☐ Second helping of dessert
☐ Stress relief	☐ Deodorant	☐ A guilty pleasure	☐ A brisk walk
☐ Family dinner	☐ An apology	☐ A primal scream	☐ A "Please"
☐ Beds all made	☐ Lottery win	☐ A clean kitchen	☐ A "Thank you"
☐ A pick-me-up	☐ A six-pack	☐ More chocolate	☐ A present
☐ Fireman fantasy	☐ Dust bunny eradication	☐ A foot rub	☐ My prince to come
☐ The toothpaste capped	☐ A parking spot	☐ Chores completed	☐ A big bowl of ice cream
☐ A good hair day	☐ No tears	☐ Snuggle time	☐ A serenade
☐ Less laundry	☐ Stain-free day	☐ A good laugh	☐ Grace under pressure
☐ Window-shopping	☐ A haiku	☐ Clean sheets	☐ Mind over matter
☐ Complete obedience	☐ Cuddling	☐ A glass of bubbly	☐ Good will
☐ A chuckle	☐ Coddling	☐ Better neighbors	☐ Flowers
☐ Clean children	☐ A blowout	☐ To hear I'm cool	☐ A miracle
☐ A sincere compliment	☐ An empty dishwasher	☐ To hear I'm hot	☐ Some "me" time
☐ Mani-pedi	☐ You to put on a sweater	☐ Yoga	☐ A good cry
☐ A shoulder to cry on	☐ A nap	☐ Validation	☐ Girl's night out
☐ A random thoughtful act	☐ More help	☐ Breakfast in bed	☐ Romantic dinner
☐ To feel like a million bucks	☐ Complete silence	☐ Control of remote	☐ Full-time help
☐ To look like a million bucks	☐ Extra cheese	☐ A neck rub	☐ Just a little appreciation
☐ A million bucks	☐ A bra that fits	☐ A big smile	☐ Just you

☐ **PLEASE**　　☐ **PRETTY PLEASE**　　☐ **THANK YOU**　　☐ **OR ELSE**

SIGNATURE (ACTUAL NAME OF MOTHER)

MONTH	DAY	YEAR

KNOCKKNOCKSTUFF.COM ■ © 2014 WHO'S THERE INC.

"IS IT REALLY SO MUCH TO ASK?"

THINGS MOM REALLY, REALLY, REALLY NEEDS

☐ **SOON**   ☐ **TODAY**   ☐ **RIGHT NOW**   ☐ **FROM NOW ON**

SOON	TODAY	RIGHT NOW	FROM NOW ON
☐ A break	☐ For you to read my mind	☐ Candlelight	☐ Movie night
☐ Less whine	☐ An aspirin	☐ Space	☐ A side of fries
☐ More wine	☐ Some respect	☐ A well-stocked fridge	☐ Some lovin'
☐ Your love	☐ Pizza, toppings my choice	☐ Commiseration	☐ A chauffeur
☐ Chocolate	☐ A good book	☐ To sleep in	☐ Inside voices
☐ A vacation	☐ Work-life balance	☐ A margarita	☐ A little more help
☐ Peace	☐ For you to make dinner	☐ Tantrum absence	☐ Vim
☐ Quiet	☐ A little enthusiasm	☐ The toilet seat down	☐ Vigor
☐ Peace and quiet	☐ To recapture my youth	☐ Someone to take out dog	☐ A good babysitter
☐ A date night	☐ Alone time	☐ Someone to bring in cat	☐ Soft lights
☐ The toilet paper replaced	☐ Alone time in bathroom	☐ A makeover	☐ Soft music
☐ Pampering	☐ Someone to admit I'm right	☐ Costume drama on DVR	☐ Clean clothes
☐ A kiss	☐ A shopping spree	☐ Reality TV on DVR	☐ Time to read
☐ A hug	☐ Attitude of gratitude	☐ Punctuality	☐ A day without dieting
☐ A bear hug	☐ Pie	☐ Endorphin rush	☐ Calm
☐ Someone to listen	☐ A massage	☐ Personal shopper	☐ A friendly phone call
☐ Takeout	☐ An ego massage	☐ Personal schlepper	☐ A day off
☐ A little help	☐ All the answers	☐ A mate to that sock	☐ A smidgen of kindness
☐ To fit into those jeans	☐ Any answer	☐ Time to reflect	☐ A good workout
☐ Privacy	☐ Sweet nothings	☐ A little consideration	☐ A new job
☐ A love note	☐ Personal trainer	☐ Spa day	☐ Even more wine
☐ No complaints	☐ Personal assistant	☐ To be fed grapes	☐ Utter devotion
☐ Hot coffee	☐ A cup of tea	☐ A stiff one	☐ Cupcakes
☐ A hot bath	☐ Therapy	☐ Mother's little helper	☐ Thermostat control
☐ A cold shower	☐ A good night's sleep	☐ A pep talk	☐ A cold drink
☐ Some good gossip	☐ Jewelry	☐ Fewer interruptions	☐ Inner peace
☐ A day in pajamas	☐ To be the center of attention	☐ To win	☐ A day without poop
☐ A day out of sweats	☐ To sit down for a minute	☐ A sugar fix	☐ Sympathy
☐ New shoes	☐ A happy child	☐ Well-behaved inner child	☐ Empathy
☐ A bit of effort	☐ A happy spouse	☐ Well-behaved children	☐ A comfy chair
☐ Barf-free clothing	☐ Praise for my intellect	☐ To get outside	☐ Second helping of dessert
☐ Stress relief	☐ Deodorant	☐ A guilty pleasure	☐ A brisk walk
☐ Family dinner	☐ An apology	☐ A primal scream	☐ A "Please"
☐ Beds all made	☐ Lottery win	☐ A clean kitchen	☐ A "Thank you"
☐ A pick-me-up	☐ A six-pack	☐ More chocolate	☐ A present
☐ Fireman fantasy	☐ Dust bunny eradication	☐ A foot rub	☐ My prince to come
☐ The toothpaste capped	☐ A parking spot	☐ Chores completed	☐ A big bowl of ice cream
☐ A good hair day	☐ No tears	☐ Snuggle time	☐ A serenade
☐ Less laundry	☐ Stain-free day	☐ A good laugh	☐ Grace under pressure
☐ Window-shopping	☐ A haiku	☐ Clean sheets	☐ Mind over matter
☐ Complete obedience	☐ Cuddling	☐ A glass of bubbly	☐ Good will
☐ A chuckle	☐ Coddling	☐ Better neighbors	☐ Flowers
☐ Clean children	☐ A blowout	☐ To hear I'm cool	☐ A miracle
☐ A sincere compliment	☐ An empty dishwasher	☐ To hear I'm hot	☐ Some "me" time
☐ Mani-pedi	☐ You to put on a sweater	☐ Yoga	☐ A good cry
☐ A shoulder to cry on	☐ A nap	☐ Validation	☐ Girl's night out
☐ A random thoughtful act	☐ More help	☐ Breakfast in bed	☐ Romantic dinner
☐ To feel like a million bucks	☐ Complete silence	☐ Control of remote	☐ Full-time help
☐ To look like a million bucks	☐ Extra cheese	☐ A neck rub	☐ Just a little appreciation
☐ A million bucks	☐ A bra that fits	☐ A big smile	☐ Just you

☐ **PLEASE**   ☐ **PRETTY PLEASE**   ☐ **THANK YOU**   ☐ **OR ELSE**

SIGNATURE (ACTUAL NAME OF MOTHER)

MONTH   DAY   YEAR

"IS IT REALLY SO MUCH TO ASK?"

THINGS MOM REALLY, REALLY, REALLY NEEDS

☐ **SOON**   ☐ **TODAY**   ☐ **RIGHT NOW**   ☐ **FROM NOW ON**

SOON	TODAY	RIGHT NOW	FROM NOW ON
☐ A break	☐ For you to read my mind	☐ Candlelight	☐ Movie night
☐ Less whine	☐ An aspirin	☐ Space	☐ A side of fries
☐ More wine	☐ Some respect	☐ A well-stocked fridge	☐ Some lovin'
☐ Your love	☐ Pizza, toppings my choice	☐ Commiseration	☐ A chauffeur
☐ Chocolate	☐ A good book	☐ To sleep in	☐ Inside voices
☐ A vacation	☐ Work-life balance	☐ A margarita	☐ A little more help
☐ Peace	☐ For you to make dinner	☐ Tantrum absence	☐ Vim
☐ Quiet	☐ A little enthusiasm	☐ The toilet seat down	☐ Vigor
☐ Peace and quiet	☐ To recapture my youth	☐ Someone to take out dog	☐ A good babysitter
☐ A date night	☐ Alone time	☐ Someone to bring in cat	☐ Soft lights
☐ The toilet paper replaced	☐ Alone time in bathroom	☐ A makeover	☐ Soft music
☐ Pampering	☐ Someone to admit I'm right	☐ Costume drama on DVR	☐ Clean clothes
☐ A kiss	☐ A shopping spree	☐ Reality TV on DVR	☐ Time to read
☐ A hug	☐ Attitude of gratitude	☐ Punctuality	☐ A day without dieting
☐ A bear hug	☐ Pie	☐ Endorphin rush	☐ Calm
☐ Someone to listen	☐ A massage	☐ Personal shopper	☐ A friendly phone call
☐ Takeout	☐ An ego massage	☐ Personal schlepper	☐ A day off
☐ A little help	☐ All the answers	☐ A mate to that sock	☐ A smidgen of kindness
☐ To fit into those jeans	☐ Any answer	☐ Time to reflect	☐ A good workout
☐ Privacy	☐ Sweet nothings	☐ A little consideration	☐ A new job
☐ A love note	☐ Personal trainer	☐ Spa day	☐ Even more wine
☐ No complaints	☐ Personal assistant	☐ To be fed grapes	☐ Utter devotion
☐ Hot coffee	☐ A cup of tea	☐ A stiff one	☐ Cupcakes
☐ A hot bath	☐ Therapy	☐ Mother's little helper	☐ Thermostat control
☐ A cold shower	☐ A good night's sleep	☐ A pep talk	☐ A cold drink
☐ Some good gossip	☐ Jewelry	☐ Fewer interruptions	☐ Inner peace
☐ A day in pajamas	☐ To be the center of attention	☐ To win	☐ A day without poop
☐ A day out of sweats	☐ To sit down for a minute	☐ A sugar fix	☐ Sympathy
☐ New shoes	☐ A happy child	☐ Well-behaved inner child	☐ Empathy
☐ A bit of effort	☐ A happy spouse	☐ Well-behaved children	☐ A comfy chair
☐ Barf-free clothing	☐ Praise for my intellect	☐ To get outside	☐ Second helping of dessert
☐ Stress relief	☐ Deodorant	☐ A guilty pleasure	☐ A brisk walk
☐ Family dinner	☐ An apology	☐ A primal scream	☐ A "Please"
☐ Beds all made	☐ Lottery win	☐ A clean kitchen	☐ A "Thank you"
☐ A pick-me-up	☐ A six-pack	☐ More chocolate	☐ A present
☐ Fireman fantasy	☐ Dust bunny eradication	☐ A foot rub	☐ My prince to come
☐ The toothpaste capped	☐ A parking spot	☐ Chores completed	☐ A big bowl of ice cream
☐ A good hair day	☐ No tears	☐ Snuggle time	☐ A serenade
☐ Less laundry	☐ Stain-free day	☐ A good laugh	☐ Grace under pressure
☐ Window-shopping	☐ A haiku	☐ Clean sheets	☐ Mind over matter
☐ Complete obedience	☐ Cuddling	☐ A glass of bubbly	☐ Good will
☐ A chuckle	☐ Coddling	☐ Better neighbors	☐ Flowers
☐ Clean children	☐ A blowout	☐ To hear I'm cool	☐ A miracle
☐ A sincere compliment	☐ An empty dishwasher	☐ To hear I'm hot	☐ Some "me" time
☐ Mani-pedi	☐ You to put on a sweater	☐ Yoga	☐ A good cry
☐ A shoulder to cry on	☐ A nap	☐ Validation	☐ Girl's night out
☐ A random thoughtful act	☐ More help	☐ Breakfast in bed	☐ Romantic dinner
☐ To feel like a million bucks	☐ Complete silence	☐ Control of remote	☐ Full-time help
☐ To look like a million bucks	☐ Extra cheese	☐ A neck rub	☐ Just a little appreciation
☐ A million bucks	☐ A bra that fits	☐ A big smile	☐ Just you

☐ **PLEASE**   ☐ **PRETTY PLEASE**   ☐ **THANK YOU**   ☐ **OR ELSE**

SIGNATURE (ACTUAL NAME OF MOTHER)	MONTH	DAY	YEAR

"IS IT REALLY SO MUCH TO ASK?"

THINGS MOM REALLY, REALLY, REALLY NEEDS

☐ **SOON**   ☐ **TODAY**   ☐ **RIGHT NOW**   ☐ **FROM NOW ON**

☐ A break	☐ For you to read my mind	☐ Candlelight	☐ Movie night
☐ Less whine	☐ An aspirin	☐ Space	☐ A side of fries
☐ More wine	☐ Some respect	☐ A well-stocked fridge	☐ Some lovin'
☐ Your love	☐ Pizza, toppings my choice	☐ Commiseration	☐ A chauffeur
☐ Chocolate	☐ A good book	☐ To sleep in	☐ Inside voices
☐ A vacation	☐ Work-life balance	☐ A margarita	☐ A little more help
☐ Peace	☐ For you to make dinner	☐ Tantrum absence	☐ Vim
☐ Quiet	☐ A little enthusiasm	☐ The toilet seat down	☐ Vigor
☐ Peace and quiet	☐ To recapture my youth	☐ Someone to take out dog	☐ A good babysitter
☐ A date night	☐ Alone time	☐ Someone to bring in cat	☐ Soft lights
☐ The toilet paper replaced	☐ Alone time in bathroom	☐ A makeover	☐ Soft music
☐ Pampering	☐ Someone to admit I'm right	☐ Costume drama on DVR	☐ Clean clothes
☐ A kiss	☐ A shopping spree	☐ Reality TV on DVR	☐ Time to read
☐ A hug	☐ Attitude of gratitude	☐ Punctuality	☐ A day without dieting
☐ A bear hug	☐ Pie	☐ Endorphin rush	☐ Calm
☐ Someone to listen	☐ A massage	☐ Personal shopper	☐ A friendly phone call
☐ Takeout	☐ An ego massage	☐ Personal schlepper	☐ A day off
☐ A little help	☐ All the answers	☐ A mate to that sock	☐ A smidgen of kindness
☐ To fit into those jeans	☐ Any answer	☐ Time to reflect	☐ A good workout
☐ Privacy	☐ Sweet nothings	☐ A little consideration	☐ A new job
☐ A love note	☐ Personal trainer	☐ Spa day	☐ Even more wine
☐ No complaints	☐ Personal assistant	☐ To be fed grapes	☐ Utter devotion
☐ Hot coffee	☐ A cup of tea	☐ A stiff one	☐ Cupcakes
☐ A hot bath	☐ Therapy	☐ Mother's little helper	☐ Thermostat control
☐ A cold shower	☐ A good night's sleep	☐ A pep talk	☐ A cold drink
☐ Some good gossip	☐ Jewelry	☐ Fewer interruptions	☐ Inner peace
☐ A day in pajamas	☐ To be the center of attention	☐ To win	☐ A day without poop
☐ A day out of sweats	☐ To sit down for a minute	☐ A sugar fix	☐ Sympathy
☐ New shoes	☐ A happy child	☐ Well-behaved inner child	☐ Empathy
☐ A bit of effort	☐ A happy spouse	☐ Well-behaved children	☐ A comfy chair
☐ Barf-free clothing	☐ Praise for my intellect	☐ To get outside	☐ Second helping of dessert
☐ Stress relief	☐ Deodorant	☐ A guilty pleasure	☐ A brisk walk
☐ Family dinner	☐ An apology	☐ A primal scream	☐ A "Please"
☐ Beds all made	☐ Lottery win	☐ A clean kitchen	☐ A "Thank you"
☐ A pick-me-up	☐ A six-pack	☐ More chocolate	☐ A present
☐ Fireman fantasy	☐ Dust bunny eradication	☐ A foot rub	☐ My prince to come
☐ The toothpaste capped	☐ A parking spot	☐ Chores completed	☐ A big bowl of ice cream
☐ A good hair day	☐ No tears	☐ Snuggle time	☐ A serenade
☐ Less laundry	☐ Stain-free day	☐ A good laugh	☐ Grace under pressure
☐ Window-shopping	☐ A haiku	☐ Clean sheets	☐ Mind over matter
☐ Complete obedience	☐ Cuddling	☐ A glass of bubbly	☐ Good will
☐ A chuckle	☐ Coddling	☐ Better neighbors	☐ Flowers
☐ Clean children	☐ A blowout	☐ To hear I'm cool	☐ A miracle
☐ A sincere compliment	☐ An empty dishwasher	☐ To hear I'm hot	☐ Some "me" time
☐ Mani-pedi	☐ You to put on a sweater	☐ Yoga	☐ A good cry
☐ A shoulder to cry on	☐ A nap	☐ Validation	☐ Girl's night out
☐ A random thoughtful act	☐ More help	☐ Breakfast in bed	☐ Romantic dinner
☐ To feel like a million bucks	☐ Complete silence	☐ Control of remote	☐ Full-time help
☐ To look like a million bucks	☐ Extra cheese	☐ A neck rub	☐ Just a little appreciation
☐ A million bucks	☐ A bra that fits	☐ A big smile	☐ Just you

☐ **PLEASE**   ☐ **PRETTY PLEASE**   ☐ **THANK YOU**   ☐ **OR ELSE**

SIGNATURE (ACTUAL NAME OF MOTHER)

| MONTH | DAY | YEAR |

"IS IT REALLY SO MUCH TO ASK?"

THINGS MOM REALLY, REALLY, REALLY NEEDS

☐ **SOON**   ☐ **TODAY**   ☐ **RIGHT NOW**   ☐ **FROM NOW ON**

SOON	TODAY	RIGHT NOW	FROM NOW ON
☐ A break	☐ For you to read my mind	☐ Candlelight	☐ Movie night
☐ Less whine	☐ An aspirin	☐ Space	☐ A side of fries
☐ More wine	☐ Some respect	☐ A well-stocked fridge	☐ Some lovin'
☐ Your love	☐ Pizza, toppings my choice	☐ Commiseration	☐ A chauffeur
☐ Chocolate	☐ A good book	☐ To sleep in	☐ Inside voices
☐ A vacation	☐ Work-life balance	☐ A margarita	☐ A little more help
☐ Peace	☐ For you to make dinner	☐ Tantrum absence	☐ Vim
☐ Quiet	☐ A little enthusiasm	☐ The toilet seat down	☐ Vigor
☐ Peace and quiet	☐ To recapture my youth	☐ Someone to take out dog	☐ A good babysitter
☐ A date night	☐ Alone time	☐ Someone to bring in cat	☐ Soft lights
☐ The toilet paper replaced	☐ Alone time in bathroom	☐ A makeover	☐ Soft music
☐ Pampering	☐ Someone to admit I'm right	☐ Costume drama on DVR	☐ Clean clothes
☐ A kiss	☐ A shopping spree	☐ Reality TV on DVR	☐ Time to read
☐ A hug	☐ Attitude of gratitude	☐ Punctuality	☐ A day without dieting
☐ A bear hug	☐ Pie	☐ Endorphin rush	☐ Calm
☐ Someone to listen	☐ A massage	☐ Personal shopper	☐ A friendly phone call
☐ Takeout	☐ An ego massage	☐ Personal schlepper	☐ A day off
☐ A little help	☐ All the answers	☐ A mate to that sock	☐ A smidgen of kindness
☐ To fit into those jeans	☐ Any answer	☐ Time to reflect	☐ A good workout
☐ Privacy	☐ Sweet nothings	☐ A little consideration	☐ A new job
☐ A love note	☐ Personal trainer	☐ Spa day	☐ Even more wine
☐ No complaints	☐ Personal assistant	☐ To be fed grapes	☐ Utter devotion
☐ Hot coffee	☐ A cup of tea	☐ A stiff one	☐ Cupcakes
☐ A hot bath	☐ Therapy	☐ Mother's little helper	☐ Thermostat control
☐ A cold shower	☐ A good night's sleep	☐ A pep talk	☐ A cold drink
☐ Some good gossip	☐ Jewelry	☐ Fewer interruptions	☐ Inner peace
☐ A day in pajamas	☐ To be the center of attention	☐ To win	☐ A day without poop
☐ A day out of sweats	☐ To sit down for a minute	☐ A sugar fix	☐ Sympathy
☐ New shoes	☐ A happy child	☐ Well-behaved inner child	☐ Empathy
☐ A bit of effort	☐ A happy spouse	☐ Well-behaved children	☐ A comfy chair
☐ Barf-free clothing	☐ Praise for my intellect	☐ To get outside	☐ Second helping of dessert
☐ Stress relief	☐ Deodorant	☐ A guilty pleasure	☐ A brisk walk
☐ Family dinner	☐ An apology	☐ A primal scream	☐ A "Please"
☐ Beds all made	☐ Lottery win	☐ A clean kitchen	☐ A "Thank you"
☐ A pick-me-up	☐ A six-pack	☐ More chocolate	☐ A present
☐ Fireman fantasy	☐ Dust bunny eradication	☐ A foot rub	☐ My prince to come
☐ The toothpaste capped	☐ A parking spot	☐ Chores completed	☐ A big bowl of ice cream
☐ A good hair day	☐ No tears	☐ Snuggle time	☐ A serenade
☐ Less laundry	☐ Stain-free day	☐ A good laugh	☐ Grace under pressure
☐ Window-shopping	☐ A haiku	☐ Clean sheets	☐ Mind over matter
☐ Complete obedience	☐ Cuddling	☐ A glass of bubbly	☐ Good will
☐ A chuckle	☐ Coddling	☐ Better neighbors	☐ Flowers
☐ Clean children	☐ A blowout	☐ To hear I'm cool	☐ A miracle
☐ A sincere compliment	☐ An empty dishwasher	☐ To hear I'm hot	☐ Some "me" time
☐ Mani-pedi	☐ You to put on a sweater	☐ Yoga	☐ A good cry
☐ A shoulder to cry on	☐ A nap	☐ Validation	☐ Girl's night out
☐ A random thoughtful act	☐ More help	☐ Breakfast in bed	☐ Romantic dinner
☐ To feel like a million bucks	☐ Complete silence	☐ Control of remote	☐ Full-time help
☐ To look like a million bucks	☐ Extra cheese	☐ A neck rub	☐ Just a little appreciation
☐ A million bucks	☐ A bra that fits	☐ A big smile	☐ Just you

☐ **PLEASE**   ☐ **PRETTY PLEASE**   ☐ **THANK YOU**   ☐ **OR ELSE**

SIGNATURE (ACTUAL NAME OF MOTHER)   MONTH   DAY   YEAR

"IS IT REALLY SO MUCH TO ASK?"

THINGS MOM REALLY, REALLY, REALLY NEEDS

☐ **SOON**   ☐ **TODAY**   ☐ **RIGHT NOW**   ☐ **FROM NOW ON**

☐ A break	☐ For you to read my mind	☐ Candlelight	☐ Movie night
☐ Less whine	☐ An aspirin	☐ Space	☐ A side of fries
☐ More wine	☐ Some respect	☐ A well-stocked fridge	☐ Some lovin'
☐ Your love	☐ Pizza, toppings my choice	☐ Commiseration	☐ A chauffeur
☐ Chocolate	☐ A good book	☐ To sleep in	☐ Inside voices
☐ A vacation	☐ Work-life balance	☐ A margarita	☐ A little more help
☐ Peace	☐ For you to make dinner	☐ Tantrum absence	☐ Vim
☐ Quiet	☐ A little enthusiasm	☐ The toilet seat down	☐ Vigor
☐ Peace and quiet	☐ To recapture my youth	☐ Someone to take out dog	☐ A good babysitter
☐ A date night	☐ Alone time	☐ Someone to bring in cat	☐ Soft lights
☐ The toilet paper replaced	☐ Alone time in bathroom	☐ A makeover	☐ Soft music
☐ Pampering	☐ Someone to admit I'm right	☐ Costume drama on DVR	☐ Clean clothes
☐ A kiss	☐ A shopping spree	☐ Reality TV on DVR	☐ Time to read
☐ A hug	☐ Attitude of gratitude	☐ Punctuality	☐ A day without dieting
☐ A bear hug	☐ Pie	☐ Endorphin rush	☐ Calm
☐ Someone to listen	☐ A massage	☐ Personal shopper	☐ A friendly phone call
☐ Takeout	☐ An ego massage	☐ Personal schlepper	☐ A day off
☐ A little help	☐ All the answers	☐ A mate to that sock	☐ A smidgen of kindness
☐ To fit into those jeans	☐ Any answer	☐ Time to reflect	☐ A good workout
☐ Privacy	☐ Sweet nothings	☐ A little consideration	☐ A new job
☐ A love note	☐ Personal trainer	☐ Spa day	☐ Even more wine
☐ No complaints	☐ Personal assistant	☐ To be fed grapes	☐ Utter devotion
☐ Hot coffee	☐ A cup of tea	☐ A stiff one	☐ Cupcakes
☐ A hot bath	☐ Therapy	☐ Mother's little helper	☐ Thermostat control
☐ A cold shower	☐ A good night's sleep	☐ A pep talk	☐ A cold drink
☐ Some good gossip	☐ Jewelry	☐ Fewer interruptions	☐ Inner peace
☐ A day in pajamas	☐ To be the center of attention	☐ To win	☐ A day without poop
☐ A day out of sweats	☐ To sit down for a minute	☐ A sugar fix	☐ Sympathy
☐ New shoes	☐ A happy child	☐ Well-behaved inner child	☐ Empathy
☐ A bit of effort	☐ A happy spouse	☐ Well-behaved children	☐ A comfy chair
☐ Barf-free clothing	☐ Praise for my intellect	☐ To get outside	☐ Second helping of dessert
☐ Stress relief	☐ Deodorant	☐ A guilty pleasure	☐ A brisk walk
☐ Family dinner	☐ An apology	☐ A primal scream	☐ A "Please"
☐ Beds all made	☐ Lottery win	☐ A clean kitchen	☐ A "Thank you"
☐ A pick-me-up	☐ A six-pack	☐ More chocolate	☐ A present
☐ Fireman fantasy	☐ Dust bunny eradication	☐ A foot rub	☐ My prince to come
☐ The toothpaste capped	☐ A parking spot	☐ Chores completed	☐ A big bowl of ice cream
☐ A good hair day	☐ No tears	☐ Snuggle time	☐ A serenade
☐ Less laundry	☐ Stain-free day	☐ A good laugh	☐ Grace under pressure
☐ Window-shopping	☐ A haiku	☐ Clean sheets	☐ Mind over matter
☐ Complete obedience	☐ Cuddling	☐ A glass of bubbly	☐ Good will
☐ A chuckle	☐ Coddling	☐ Better neighbors	☐ Flowers
☐ Clean children	☐ A blowout	☐ To hear I'm cool	☐ A miracle
☐ A sincere compliment	☐ An empty dishwasher	☐ To hear I'm hot	☐ Some "me" time
☐ Mani-pedi	☐ You to put on a sweater	☐ Yoga	☐ A good cry
☐ A shoulder to cry on	☐ A nap	☐ Validation	☐ Girl's night out
☐ A random thoughtful act	☐ More help	☐ Breakfast in bed	☐ Romantic dinner
☐ To feel like a million bucks	☐ Complete silence	☐ Control of remote	☐ Full-time help
☐ To look like a million bucks	☐ Extra cheese	☐ A neck rub	☐ Just a little appreciation
☐ A million bucks	☐ A bra that fits	☐ A big smile	☐ Just you

☐ **PLEASE**   ☐ **PRETTY PLEASE**   ☐ **THANK YOU**   ☐ **OR ELSE**

SIGNATURE (ACTUAL NAME OF MOTHER)   MONTH : DAY : YEAR

"IS IT REALLY SO MUCH TO ASK?"

THINGS MOM REALLY, REALLY, REALLY NEEDS

☐ **SOON** ☐ **TODAY** ☐ **RIGHT NOW** ☐ **FROM NOW ON**

SOON	TODAY	RIGHT NOW	FROM NOW ON
☐ A break	☐ For you to read my mind	☐ Candlelight	☐ Movie night
☐ Less whine	☐ An aspirin	☐ Space	☐ A side of fries
☐ More wine	☐ Some respect	☐ A well-stocked fridge	☐ Some lovin'
☐ Your love	☐ Pizza, toppings my choice	☐ Commiseration	☐ A chauffeur
☐ Chocolate	☐ A good book	☐ To sleep in	☐ Inside voices
☐ A vacation	☐ Work-life balance	☐ A margarita	☐ A little more help
☐ Peace	☐ For you to make dinner	☐ Tantrum absence	☐ Vim
☐ Quiet	☐ A little enthusiasm	☐ The toilet seat down	☐ Vigor
☐ Peace and quiet	☐ To recapture my youth	☐ Someone to take out dog	☐ A good babysitter
☐ A date night	☐ Alone time	☐ Someone to bring in cat	☐ Soft lights
☐ The toilet paper replaced	☐ Alone time in bathroom	☐ A makeover	☐ Soft music
☐ Pampering	☐ Someone to admit I'm right	☐ Costume drama on DVR	☐ Clean clothes
☐ A kiss	☐ A shopping spree	☐ Reality TV on DVR	☐ Time to read
☐ A hug	☐ Attitude of gratitude	☐ Punctuality	☐ A day without dieting
☐ A bear hug	☐ Pie	☐ Endorphin rush	☐ Calm
☐ Someone to listen	☐ A massage	☐ Personal shopper	☐ A friendly phone call
☐ Takeout	☐ An ego massage	☐ Personal schlepper	☐ A day off
☐ A little help	☐ All the answers	☐ A mate to that sock	☐ A smidgen of kindness
☐ To fit into those jeans	☐ Any answer	☐ Time to reflect	☐ A good workout
☐ Privacy	☐ Sweet nothings	☐ A little consideration	☐ A new job
☐ A love note	☐ Personal trainer	☐ Spa day	☐ Even more wine
☐ No complaints	☐ Personal assistant	☐ To be fed grapes	☐ Utter devotion
☐ Hot coffee	☐ A cup of tea	☐ A stiff one	☐ Cupcakes
☐ A hot bath	☐ Therapy	☐ Mother's little helper	☐ Thermostat control
☐ A cold shower	☐ A good night's sleep	☐ A pep talk	☐ A cold drink
☐ Some good gossip	☐ Jewelry	☐ Fewer interruptions	☐ Inner peace
☐ A day in pajamas	☐ To be the center of attention	☐ To win	☐ A day without poop
☐ A day out of sweats	☐ To sit down for a minute	☐ A sugar fix	☐ Sympathy
☐ New shoes	☐ A happy child	☐ Well-behaved inner child	☐ Empathy
☐ A bit of effort	☐ A happy spouse	☐ Well-behaved children	☐ A comfy chair
☐ Barf-free clothing	☐ Praise for my intellect	☐ To get outside	☐ Second helping of dessert
☐ Stress relief	☐ Deodorant	☐ A guilty pleasure	☐ A brisk walk
☐ Family dinner	☐ An apology	☐ A primal scream	☐ A "Please"
☐ Beds all made	☐ Lottery win	☐ A clean kitchen	☐ A "Thank you"
☐ A pick-me-up	☐ A six-pack	☐ More chocolate	☐ A present
☐ Fireman fantasy	☐ Dust bunny eradication	☐ A foot rub	☐ My prince to come
☐ The toothpaste capped	☐ A parking spot	☐ Chores completed	☐ A big bowl of ice cream
☐ A good hair day	☐ No tears	☐ Snuggle time	☐ A serenade
☐ Less laundry	☐ Stain-free day	☐ A good laugh	☐ Grace under pressure
☐ Window-shopping	☐ A haiku	☐ Clean sheets	☐ Mind over matter
☐ Complete obedience	☐ Cuddling	☐ A glass of bubbly	☐ Good will
☐ A chuckle	☐ Coddling	☐ Better neighbors	☐ Flowers
☐ Clean children	☐ A blowout	☐ To hear I'm cool	☐ A miracle
☐ A sincere compliment	☐ An empty dishwasher	☐ To hear I'm hot	☐ Some "me" time
☐ Mani-pedi	☐ You to put on a sweater	☐ Yoga	☐ A good cry
☐ A shoulder to cry on	☐ A nap	☐ Validation	☐ Girl's night out
☐ A random thoughtful act	☐ More help	☐ Breakfast in bed	☐ Romantic dinner
☐ To feel like a million bucks	☐ Complete silence	☐ Control of remote	☐ Full-time help
☐ To look like a million bucks	☐ Extra cheese	☐ A neck rub	☐ Just a little appreciation
☐ A million bucks	☐ A bra that fits	☐ A big smile	☐ Just you

☐ **PLEASE** ☐ **PRETTY PLEASE** ☐ **THANK YOU** ☐ **OR ELSE**

SIGNATURE (ACTUAL NAME OF MOTHER)

| MONTH | DAY | YEAR |

"IS IT REALLY SO MUCH TO ASK?"

THINGS MOM REALLY, REALLY, REALLY NEEDS

☐ **SOON** ☐ **TODAY** ☐ **RIGHT NOW** ☐ **FROM NOW ON**

☐ A break	☐ For you to read my mind	☐ Candlelight	☐ Movie night
☐ Less whine	☐ An aspirin	☐ Space	☐ A side of fries
☐ More wine	☐ Some respect	☐ A well-stocked fridge	☐ Some lovin'
☐ Your love	☐ Pizza, toppings my choice	☐ Commiseration	☐ A chauffeur
☐ Chocolate	☐ A good book	☐ To sleep in	☐ Inside voices
☐ A vacation	☐ Work-life balance	☐ A margarita	☐ A little more help
☐ Peace	☐ For you to make dinner	☐ Tantrum absence	☐ Vim
☐ Quiet	☐ A little enthusiasm	☐ The toilet seat down	☐ Vigor
☐ Peace and quiet	☐ To recapture my youth	☐ Someone to take out dog	☐ A good babysitter
☐ A date night	☐ Alone time	☐ Someone to bring in cat	☐ Soft lights
☐ The toilet paper replaced	☐ Alone time in bathroom	☐ A makeover	☐ Soft music
☐ Pampering	☐ Someone to admit I'm right	☐ Costume drama on DVR	☐ Clean clothes
☐ A kiss	☐ A shopping spree	☐ Reality TV on DVR	☐ Time to read
☐ A hug	☐ Attitude of gratitude	☐ Punctuality	☐ A day without dieting
☐ A bear hug	☐ Pie	☐ Endorphin rush	☐ Calm
☐ Someone to listen	☐ A massage	☐ Personal shopper	☐ A friendly phone call
☐ Takeout	☐ An ego massage	☐ Personal schlepper	☐ A day off
☐ A little help	☐ All the answers	☐ A mate to that sock	☐ A smidgen of kindness
☐ To fit into those jeans	☐ Any answer	☐ Time to reflect	☐ A good workout
☐ Privacy	☐ Sweet nothings	☐ A little consideration	☐ A new job
☐ A love note	☐ Personal trainer	☐ Spa day	☐ Even more wine
☐ No complaints	☐ Personal assistant	☐ To be fed grapes	☐ Utter devotion
☐ Hot coffee	☐ A cup of tea	☐ A stiff one	☐ Cupcakes
☐ A hot bath	☐ Therapy	☐ Mother's little helper	☐ Thermostat control
☐ A cold shower	☐ A good night's sleep	☐ A pep talk	☐ A cold drink
☐ Some good gossip	☐ Jewelry	☐ Fewer interruptions	☐ Inner peace
☐ A day in pajamas	☐ To be the center of attention	☐ To win	☐ A day without poop
☐ A day out of sweats	☐ To sit down for a minute	☐ A sugar fix	☐ Sympathy
☐ New shoes	☐ A happy child	☐ Well-behaved inner child	☐ Empathy
☐ A bit of effort	☐ A happy spouse	☐ Well-behaved children	☐ A comfy chair
☐ Barf-free clothing	☐ Praise for my intellect	☐ To get outside	☐ Second helping of dessert
☐ Stress relief	☐ Deodorant	☐ A guilty pleasure	☐ A brisk walk
☐ Family dinner	☐ An apology	☐ A primal scream	☐ A "Please"
☐ Beds all made	☐ Lottery win	☐ A clean kitchen	☐ A "Thank you"
☐ A pick-me-up	☐ A six-pack	☐ More chocolate	☐ A present
☐ Fireman fantasy	☐ Dust bunny eradication	☐ A foot rub	☐ My prince to come
☐ The toothpaste capped	☐ A parking spot	☐ Chores completed	☐ A big bowl of ice cream
☐ A good hair day	☐ No tears	☐ Snuggle time	☐ A serenade
☐ Less laundry	☐ Stain-free day	☐ A good laugh	☐ Grace under pressure
☐ Window-shopping	☐ A haiku	☐ Clean sheets	☐ Mind over matter
☐ Complete obedience	☐ Cuddling	☐ A glass of bubbly	☐ Good will
☐ A chuckle	☐ Coddling	☐ Better neighbors	☐ Flowers
☐ Clean children	☐ A blowout	☐ To hear I'm cool	☐ A miracle
☐ A sincere compliment	☐ An empty dishwasher	☐ To hear I'm hot	☐ Some "me" time
☐ Mani-pedi	☐ You to put on a sweater	☐ Yoga	☐ A good cry
☐ A shoulder to cry on	☐ A nap	☐ Validation	☐ Girl's night out
☐ A random thoughtful act	☐ More help	☐ Breakfast in bed	☐ Romantic dinner
☐ To feel like a million bucks	☐ Complete silence	☐ Control of remote	☐ Full-time help
☐ To look like a million bucks	☐ Extra cheese	☐ A neck rub	☐ Just a little appreciation
☐ A million bucks	☐ A bra that fits	☐ A big smile	☐ Just you

☐ **PLEASE** ☐ **PRETTY PLEASE** ☐ **THANK YOU** ☐ **OR ELSE**

SIGNATURE (ACTUAL NAME OF MOTHER) | MONTH | DAY | YEAR

"IS IT REALLY SO MUCH TO ASK?"

THINGS MOM REALLY, REALLY, REALLY NEEDS

☐ **SOON**   ☐ **TODAY**   ☐ **RIGHT NOW**   ☐ **FROM NOW ON**

SOON	TODAY	RIGHT NOW	FROM NOW ON
☐ A break	☐ For you to read my mind	☐ Candlelight	☐ Movie night
☐ Less whine	☐ An aspirin	☐ Space	☐ A side of fries
☐ More wine	☐ Some respect	☐ A well-stocked fridge	☐ Some lovin'
☐ Your love	☐ Pizza, toppings my choice	☐ Commiseration	☐ A chauffeur
☐ Chocolate	☐ A good book	☐ To sleep in	☐ Inside voices
☐ A vacation	☐ Work-life balance	☐ A margarita	☐ A little more help
☐ Peace	☐ For you to make dinner	☐ Tantrum absence	☐ Vim
☐ Quiet	☐ A little enthusiasm	☐ The toilet seat down	☐ Vigor
☐ Peace and quiet	☐ To recapture my youth	☐ Someone to take out dog	☐ A good babysitter
☐ A date night	☐ Alone time	☐ Someone to bring in cat	☐ Soft lights
☐ The toilet paper replaced	☐ Alone time in bathroom	☐ A makeover	☐ Soft music
☐ Pampering	☐ Someone to admit I'm right	☐ Costume drama on DVR	☐ Clean clothes
☐ A kiss	☐ A shopping spree	☐ Reality TV on DVR	☐ Time to read
☐ A hug	☐ Attitude of gratitude	☐ Punctuality	☐ A day without dieting
☐ A bear hug	☐ Pie	☐ Endorphin rush	☐ Calm
☐ Someone to listen	☐ A massage	☐ Personal shopper	☐ A friendly phone call
☐ Takeout	☐ An ego massage	☐ Personal schlepper	☐ A day off
☐ A little help	☐ All the answers	☐ A mate to that sock	☐ A smidgen of kindness
☐ To fit into those jeans	☐ Any answer	☐ Time to reflect	☐ A good workout
☐ Privacy	☐ Sweet nothings	☐ A little consideration	☐ A new job
☐ A love note	☐ Personal trainer	☐ Spa day	☐ Even more wine
☐ No complaints	☐ Personal assistant	☐ To be fed grapes	☐ Utter devotion
☐ Hot coffee	☐ A cup of tea	☐ A stiff one	☐ Cupcakes
☐ A hot bath	☐ Therapy	☐ Mother's little helper	☐ Thermostat control
☐ A cold shower	☐ A good night's sleep	☐ A pep talk	☐ A cold drink
☐ Some good gossip	☐ Jewelry	☐ Fewer interruptions	☐ Inner peace
☐ A day in pajamas	☐ To be the center of attention	☐ To win	☐ A day without poop
☐ A day out of sweats	☐ To sit down for a minute	☐ A sugar fix	☐ Sympathy
☐ New shoes	☐ A happy child	☐ Well-behaved inner child	☐ Empathy
☐ A bit of effort	☐ A happy spouse	☐ Well-behaved children	☐ A comfy chair
☐ Barf-free clothing	☐ Praise for my intellect	☐ To get outside	☐ Second helping of dessert
☐ Stress relief	☐ Deodorant	☐ A guilty pleasure	☐ A brisk walk
☐ Family dinner	☐ An apology	☐ A primal scream	☐ A "Please"
☐ Beds all made	☐ Lottery win	☐ A clean kitchen	☐ A "Thank you"
☐ A pick-me-up	☐ A six-pack	☐ More chocolate	☐ A present
☐ Fireman fantasy	☐ Dust bunny eradication	☐ A foot rub	☐ My prince to come
☐ The toothpaste capped	☐ A parking spot	☐ Chores completed	☐ A big bowl of ice cream
☐ A good hair day	☐ No tears	☐ Snuggle time	☐ A serenade
☐ Less laundry	☐ Stain-free day	☐ A good laugh	☐ Grace under pressure
☐ Window-shopping	☐ A haiku	☐ Clean sheets	☐ Mind over matter
☐ Complete obedience	☐ Cuddling	☐ A glass of bubbly	☐ Good will
☐ A chuckle	☐ Coddling	☐ Better neighbors	☐ Flowers
☐ Clean children	☐ A blowout	☐ To hear I'm cool	☐ A miracle
☐ A sincere compliment	☐ An empty dishwasher	☐ To hear I'm hot	☐ Some "me" time
☐ Mani-pedi	☐ You to put on a sweater	☐ Yoga	☐ A good cry
☐ A shoulder to cry on	☐ A nap	☐ Validation	☐ Girl's night out
☐ A random thoughtful act	☐ More help	☐ Breakfast in bed	☐ Romantic dinner
☐ To feel like a million bucks	☐ Complete silence	☐ Control of remote	☐ Full-time help
☐ To look like a million bucks	☐ Extra cheese	☐ A neck rub	☐ Just a little appreciation
☐ A million bucks	☐ A bra that fits	☐ A big smile	☐ Just you

☐ **PLEASE**   ☐ **PRETTY PLEASE**   ☐ **THANK YOU**   ☐ **OR ELSE**

SIGNATURE (ACTUAL NAME OF MOTHER)   MONTH   DAY   YEAR

"IS IT REALLY SO MUCH TO ASK?"

THINGS MOM REALLY, REALLY, REALLY NEEDS

☐ SOON	☐ TODAY	☐ RIGHT NOW	☐ FROM NOW ON
☐ A break	☐ For you to read my mind	☐ Candlelight	☐ Movie night
☐ Less whine	☐ An aspirin	☐ Space	☐ A side of fries
☐ More wine	☐ Some respect	☐ A well-stocked fridge	☐ Some lovin'
☐ Your love	☐ Pizza, toppings my choice	☐ Commiseration	☐ A chauffeur
☐ Chocolate	☐ A good book	☐ To sleep in	☐ Inside voices
☐ A vacation	☐ Work-life balance	☐ A margarita	☐ A little more help
☐ Peace	☐ For you to make dinner	☐ Tantrum absence	☐ Vim
☐ Quiet	☐ A little enthusiasm	☐ The toilet seat down	☐ Vigor
☐ Peace and quiet	☐ To recapture my youth	☐ Someone to take out dog	☐ A good babysitter
☐ A date night	☐ Alone time	☐ Someone to bring in cat	☐ Soft lights
☐ The toilet paper replaced	☐ Alone time in bathroom	☐ A makeover	☐ Soft music
☐ Pampering	☐ Someone to admit I'm right	☐ Costume drama on DVR	☐ Clean clothes
☐ A kiss	☐ A shopping spree	☐ Reality TV on DVR	☐ Time to read
☐ A hug	☐ Attitude of gratitude	☐ Punctuality	☐ A day without dieting
☐ A bear hug	☐ Pie	☐ Endorphin rush	☐ Calm
☐ Someone to listen	☐ A massage	☐ Personal shopper	☐ A friendly phone call
☐ Takeout	☐ An ego massage	☐ Personal schlepper	☐ A day off
☐ A little help	☐ All the answers	☐ A mate to that sock	☐ A smidgen of kindness
☐ To fit into those jeans	☐ Any answer	☐ Time to reflect	☐ A good workout
☐ Privacy	☐ Sweet nothings	☐ A little consideration	☐ A new job
☐ A love note	☐ Personal trainer	☐ Spa day	☐ Even more wine
☐ No complaints	☐ Personal assistant	☐ To be fed grapes	☐ Utter devotion
☐ Hot coffee	☐ A cup of tea	☐ A stiff one	☐ Cupcakes
☐ A hot bath	☐ Therapy	☐ Mother's little helper	☐ Thermostat control
☐ A cold shower	☐ A good night's sleep	☐ A pep talk	☐ A cold drink
☐ Some good gossip	☐ Jewelry	☐ Fewer interruptions	☐ Inner peace
☐ A day in pajamas	☐ To be the center of attention	☐ To win	☐ A day without poop
☐ A day out of sweats	☐ To sit down for a minute	☐ A sugar fix	☐ Sympathy
☐ New shoes	☐ A happy child	☐ Well-behaved inner child	☐ Empathy
☐ A bit of effort	☐ A happy spouse	☐ Well-behaved children	☐ A comfy chair
☐ Barf-free clothing	☐ Praise for my intellect	☐ To get outside	☐ Second helping of dessert
☐ Stress relief	☐ Deodorant	☐ A guilty pleasure	☐ A brisk walk
☐ Family dinner	☐ An apology	☐ A primal scream	☐ A "Please"
☐ Beds all made	☐ Lottery win	☐ A clean kitchen	☐ A "Thank you"
☐ A pick-me-up	☐ A six-pack	☐ More chocolate	☐ A present
☐ Fireman fantasy	☐ Dust bunny eradication	☐ A foot rub	☐ My prince to come
☐ The toothpaste capped	☐ A parking spot	☐ Chores completed	☐ A big bowl of ice cream
☐ A good hair day	☐ No tears	☐ Snuggle time	☐ A serenade
☐ Less laundry	☐ Stain-free day	☐ A good laugh	☐ Grace under pressure
☐ Window-shopping	☐ A haiku	☐ Clean sheets	☐ Mind over matter
☐ Complete obedience	☐ Cuddling	☐ A glass of bubbly	☐ Good will
☐ A chuckle	☐ Coddling	☐ Better neighbors	☐ Flowers
☐ Clean children	☐ A blowout	☐ To hear I'm cool	☐ A miracle
☐ A sincere compliment	☐ An empty dishwasher	☐ To hear I'm hot	☐ Some "me" time
☐ Mani-pedi	☐ You to put on a sweater	☐ Yoga	☐ A good cry
☐ A shoulder to cry on	☐ A nap	☐ Validation	☐ Girl's night out
☐ A random thoughtful act	☐ More help	☐ Breakfast in bed	☐ Romantic dinner
☐ To feel like a million bucks	☐ Complete silence	☐ Control of remote	☐ Full-time help
☐ To look like a million bucks	☐ Extra cheese	☐ A neck rub	☐ Just a little appreciation
☐ A million bucks	☐ A bra that fits	☐ A big smile	☐ Just you

☐ PLEASE	☐ PRETTY PLEASE	☐ THANK YOU	☐ OR ELSE

	MONTH	DAY	YEAR

SIGNATURE (ACTUAL NAME OF MOTHER)

"IS IT REALLY SO MUCH TO ASK?"

THINGS MOM REALLY, REALLY, REALLY NEEDS

☐ **SOON**   ☐ **TODAY**   ☐ **RIGHT NOW**   ☐ **FROM NOW ON**

☐ A break	☐ For you to read my mind	☐ Candlelight	☐ Movie night
☐ Less whine	☐ An aspirin	☐ Space	☐ A side of fries
☐ More wine	☐ Some respect	☐ A well-stocked fridge	☐ Some lovin'
☐ Your love	☐ Pizza, toppings my choice	☐ Commiseration	☐ A chauffeur
☐ Chocolate	☐ A good book	☐ To sleep in	☐ Inside voices
☐ A vacation	☐ Work-life balance	☐ A margarita	☐ A little more help
☐ Peace	☐ For you to make dinner	☐ Tantrum absence	☐ Vim
☐ Quiet	☐ A little enthusiasm	☐ The toilet seat down	☐ Vigor
☐ Peace and quiet	☐ To recapture my youth	☐ Someone to take out dog	☐ A good babysitter
☐ A date night	☐ Alone time	☐ Someone to bring in cat	☐ Soft lights
☐ The toilet paper replaced	☐ Alone time in bathroom	☐ A makeover	☐ Soft music
☐ Pampering	☐ Someone to admit I'm right	☐ Costume drama on DVR	☐ Clean clothes
☐ A kiss	☐ A shopping spree	☐ Reality TV on DVR	☐ Time to read
☐ A hug	☐ Attitude of gratitude	☐ Punctuality	☐ A day without dieting
☐ A bear hug	☐ Pie	☐ Endorphin rush	☐ Calm
☐ Someone to listen	☐ A massage	☐ Personal shopper	☐ A friendly phone call
☐ Takeout	☐ An ego massage	☐ Personal schlepper	☐ A day off
☐ A little help	☐ All the answers	☐ A mate to that sock	☐ A smidgen of kindness
☐ To fit into those jeans	☐ Any answer	☐ Time to reflect	☐ A good workout
☐ Privacy	☐ Sweet nothings	☐ A little consideration	☐ A new job
☐ A love note	☐ Personal trainer	☐ Spa day	☐ Even more wine
☐ No complaints	☐ Personal assistant	☐ To be fed grapes	☐ Utter devotion
☐ Hot coffee	☐ A cup of tea	☐ A stiff one	☐ Cupcakes
☐ A hot bath	☐ Therapy	☐ Mother's little helper	☐ Thermostat control
☐ A cold shower	☐ A good night's sleep	☐ A pep talk	☐ A cold drink
☐ Some good gossip	☐ Jewelry	☐ Fewer interruptions	☐ Inner peace
☐ A day in pajamas	☐ To be the center of attention	☐ To win	☐ A day without poop
☐ A day out of sweats	☐ To sit down for a minute	☐ A sugar fix	☐ Sympathy
☐ New shoes	☐ A happy child	☐ Well-behaved inner child	☐ Empathy
☐ A bit of effort	☐ A happy spouse	☐ Well-behaved children	☐ A comfy chair
☐ Barf-free clothing	☐ Praise for my intellect	☐ To get outside	☐ Second helping of dessert
☐ Stress relief	☐ Deodorant	☐ A guilty pleasure	☐ A brisk walk
☐ Family dinner	☐ An apology	☐ A primal scream	☐ A "Please"
☐ Beds all made	☐ Lottery win	☐ A clean kitchen	☐ A "Thank you"
☐ A pick-me-up	☐ A six-pack	☐ More chocolate	☐ A present
☐ Fireman fantasy	☐ Dust bunny eradication	☐ A foot rub	☐ My prince to come
☐ The toothpaste capped	☐ A parking spot	☐ Chores completed	☐ A big bowl of ice cream
☐ A good hair day	☐ No tears	☐ Snuggle time	☐ A serenade
☐ Less laundry	☐ Stain-free day	☐ A good laugh	☐ Grace under pressure
☐ Window-shopping	☐ A haiku	☐ Clean sheets	☐ Mind over matter
☐ Complete obedience	☐ Cuddling	☐ A glass of bubbly	☐ Good will
☐ A chuckle	☐ Coddling	☐ Better neighbors	☐ Flowers
☐ Clean children	☐ A blowout	☐ To hear I'm cool	☐ A miracle
☐ A sincere compliment	☐ An empty dishwasher	☐ To hear I'm hot	☐ Some "me" time
☐ Mani-pedi	☐ You to put on a sweater	☐ Yoga	☐ A good cry
☐ A shoulder to cry on	☐ A nap	☐ Validation	☐ Girl's night out
☐ A random thoughtful act	☐ More help	☐ Breakfast in bed	☐ Romantic dinner
☐ To feel like a million bucks	☐ Complete silence	☐ Control of remote	☐ Full-time help
☐ To look like a million bucks	☐ Extra cheese	☐ A neck rub	☐ Just a little appreciation
☐ A million bucks	☐ A bra that fits	☐ A big smile	☐ Just you

☐ **PLEASE**   ☐ **PRETTY PLEASE**   ☐ **THANK YOU**   ☐ **OR ELSE**

SIGNATURE (ACTUAL NAME OF MOTHER)   MONTH | DAY | YEAR

"IS IT REALLY SO MUCH TO ASK?"

THINGS MOM REALLY, REALLY, REALLY NEEDS

☐ **SOON** ☐ **TODAY** ☐ **RIGHT NOW** ☐ **FROM NOW ON**

☐ A break	☐ For you to read my mind	☐ Candlelight	☐ Movie night
☐ Less whine	☐ An aspirin	☐ Space	☐ A side of fries
☐ More wine	☐ Some respect	☐ A well-stocked fridge	☐ Some lovin'
☐ Your love	☐ Pizza, toppings my choice	☐ Commiseration	☐ A chauffeur
☐ Chocolate	☐ A good book	☐ To sleep in	☐ Inside voices
☐ A vacation	☐ Work-life balance	☐ A margarita	☐ A little more help
☐ Peace	☐ For you to make dinner	☐ Tantrum absence	☐ Vim
☐ Quiet	☐ A little enthusiasm	☐ The toilet seat down	☐ Vigor
☐ Peace and quiet	☐ To recapture my youth	☐ Someone to take out dog	☐ A good babysitter
☐ A date night	☐ Alone time	☐ Someone to bring in cat	☐ Soft lights
☐ The toilet paper replaced	☐ Alone time in bathroom	☐ A makeover	☐ Soft music
☐ Pampering	☐ Someone to admit I'm right	☐ Costume drama on DVR	☐ Clean clothes
☐ A kiss	☐ A shopping spree	☐ Reality TV on DVR	☐ Time to read
☐ A hug	☐ Attitude of gratitude	☐ Punctuality	☐ A day without dieting
☐ A bear hug	☐ Pie	☐ Endorphin rush	☐ Calm
☐ Someone to listen	☐ A massage	☐ Personal shopper	☐ A friendly phone call
☐ Takeout	☐ An ego massage	☐ Personal schlepper	☐ A day off
☐ A little help	☐ All the answers	☐ A mate to that sock	☐ A smidgen of kindness
☐ To fit into those jeans	☐ Any answer	☐ Time to reflect	☐ A good workout
☐ Privacy	☐ Sweet nothings	☐ A little consideration	☐ A new job
☐ A love note	☐ Personal trainer	☐ Spa day	☐ Even more wine
☐ No complaints	☐ Personal assistant	☐ To be fed grapes	☐ Utter devotion
☐ Hot coffee	☐ A cup of tea	☐ A stiff one	☐ Cupcakes
☐ A hot bath	☐ Therapy	☐ Mother's little helper	☐ Thermostat control
☐ A cold shower	☐ A good night's sleep	☐ A pep talk	☐ A cold drink
☐ Some good gossip	☐ Jewelry	☐ Fewer interruptions	☐ Inner peace
☐ A day in pajamas	☐ To be the center of attention	☐ To win	☐ A day without poop
☐ A day out of sweats	☐ To sit down for a minute	☐ A sugar fix	☐ Sympathy
☐ New shoes	☐ A happy child	☐ Well-behaved inner child	☐ Empathy
☐ A bit of effort	☐ A happy spouse	☐ Well-behaved children	☐ A comfy chair
☐ Barf-free clothing	☐ Praise for my intellect	☐ To get outside	☐ Second helping of dessert
☐ Stress relief	☐ Deodorant	☐ A guilty pleasure	☐ A brisk walk
☐ Family dinner	☐ An apology	☐ A primal scream	☐ A "Please"
☐ Beds all made	☐ Lottery win	☐ A clean kitchen	☐ A "Thank you"
☐ A pick-me-up	☐ A six-pack	☐ More chocolate	☐ A present
☐ Fireman fantasy	☐ Dust bunny eradication	☐ A foot rub	☐ My prince to come
☐ The toothpaste capped	☐ A parking spot	☐ Chores completed	☐ A big bowl of ice cream
☐ A good hair day	☐ No tears	☐ Snuggle time	☐ A serenade
☐ Less laundry	☐ Stain-free day	☐ A good laugh	☐ Grace under pressure
☐ Window-shopping	☐ A haiku	☐ Clean sheets	☐ Mind over matter
☐ Complete obedience	☐ Cuddling	☐ A glass of bubbly	☐ Good will
☐ A chuckle	☐ Coddling	☐ Better neighbors	☐ Flowers
☐ Clean children	☐ A blowout	☐ To hear I'm cool	☐ A miracle
☐ A sincere compliment	☐ An empty dishwasher	☐ To hear I'm hot	☐ Some "me" time
☐ Mani-pedi	☐ You to put on a sweater	☐ Yoga	☐ A good cry
☐ A shoulder to cry on	☐ A nap	☐ Validation	☐ Girl's night out
☐ A random thoughtful act	☐ More help	☐ Breakfast in bed	☐ Romantic dinner
☐ To feel like a million bucks	☐ Complete silence	☐ Control of remote	☐ Full-time help
☐ To look like a million bucks	☐ Extra cheese	☐ A neck rub	☐ Just a little appreciation
☐ A million bucks	☐ A bra that fits	☐ A big smile	☐ Just you

☐ **PLEASE**   ☐ **PRETTY PLEASE**   ☐ **THANK YOU**   ☐ **OR ELSE**

SIGNATURE (ACTUAL NAME OF MOTHER)   MONTH   DAY   YEAR

"IS IT REALLY SO MUCH TO ASK?"

THINGS MOM REALLY, REALLY, REALLY NEEDS

☐ **SOON**   ☐ **TODAY**   ☐ **RIGHT NOW**   ☐ **FROM NOW ON**

SOON	TODAY	RIGHT NOW	FROM NOW ON
☐ A break	☐ For you to read my mind	☐ Candlelight	☐ Movie night
☐ Less whine	☐ An aspirin	☐ Space	☐ A side of fries
☐ More wine	☐ Some respect	☐ A well-stocked fridge	☐ Some lovin'
☐ Your love	☐ Pizza, toppings my choice	☐ Commiseration	☐ A chauffeur
☐ Chocolate	☐ A good book	☐ To sleep in	☐ Inside voices
☐ A vacation	☐ Work-life balance	☐ A margarita	☐ A little more help
☐ Peace	☐ For you to make dinner	☐ Tantrum absence	☐ Vim
☐ Quiet	☐ A little enthusiasm	☐ The toilet seat down	☐ Vigor
☐ Peace and quiet	☐ To recapture my youth	☐ Someone to take out dog	☐ A good babysitter
☐ A date night	☐ Alone time	☐ Someone to bring in cat	☐ Soft lights
☐ The toilet paper replaced	☐ Alone time in bathroom	☐ A makeover	☐ Soft music
☐ Pampering	☐ Someone to admit I'm right	☐ Costume drama on DVR	☐ Clean clothes
☐ A kiss	☐ A shopping spree	☐ Reality TV on DVR	☐ Time to read
☐ A hug	☐ Attitude of gratitude	☐ Punctuality	☐ A day without dieting
☐ A bear hug	☐ Pie	☐ Endorphin rush	☐ Calm
☐ Someone to listen	☐ A massage	☐ Personal shopper	☐ A friendly phone call
☐ Takeout	☐ An ego massage	☐ Personal schlepper	☐ A day off
☐ A little help	☐ All the answers	☐ A mate to that sock	☐ A smidgen of kindness
☐ To fit into those jeans	☐ Any answer	☐ Time to reflect	☐ A good workout
☐ Privacy	☐ Sweet nothings	☐ A little consideration	☐ A new job
☐ A love note	☐ Personal trainer	☐ Spa day	☐ Even more wine
☐ No complaints	☐ Personal assistant	☐ To be fed grapes	☐ Utter devotion
☐ Hot coffee	☐ A cup of tea	☐ A stiff one	☐ Cupcakes
☐ A hot bath	☐ Therapy	☐ Mother's little helper	☐ Thermostat control
☐ A cold shower	☐ A good night's sleep	☐ A pep talk	☐ A cold drink
☐ Some good gossip	☐ Jewelry	☐ Fewer interruptions	☐ Inner peace
☐ A day in pajamas	☐ To be the center of attention	☐ To win	☐ A day without poop
☐ A day out of sweats	☐ To sit down for a minute	☐ A sugar fix	☐ Sympathy
☐ New shoes	☐ A happy child	☐ Well-behaved inner child	☐ Empathy
☐ A bit of effort	☐ A happy spouse	☐ Well-behaved children	☐ A comfy chair
☐ Barf-free clothing	☐ Praise for my intellect	☐ To get outside	☐ Second helping of dessert
☐ Stress relief	☐ Deodorant	☐ A guilty pleasure	☐ A brisk walk
☐ Family dinner	☐ An apology	☐ A primal scream	☐ A "Please"
☐ Beds all made	☐ Lottery win	☐ A clean kitchen	☐ A "Thank you"
☐ A pick-me-up	☐ A six-pack	☐ More chocolate	☐ A present
☐ Fireman fantasy	☐ Dust bunny eradication	☐ A foot rub	☐ My prince to come
☐ The toothpaste capped	☐ A parking spot	☐ Chores completed	☐ A big bowl of ice cream
☐ A good hair day	☐ No tears	☐ Snuggle time	☐ A serenade
☐ Less laundry	☐ Stain-free day	☐ A good laugh	☐ Grace under pressure
☐ Window-shopping	☐ A haiku .	☐ Clean sheets	☐ Mind over matter
☐ Complete obedience	☐ Cuddling	☐ A glass of bubbly	☐ Good will
☐ A chuckle	☐ Coddling	☐ Better neighbors	☐ Flowers
☐ Clean children	☐ A blowout	☐ To hear I'm cool	☐ A miracle
☐ A sincere compliment	☐ An empty dishwasher	☐ To hear I'm hot	☐ Some "me" time
☐ Mani-pedi	☐ You to put on a sweater	☐ Yoga	☐ A good cry
☐ A shoulder to cry on	☐ A nap	☐ Validation	☐ Girl's night out
☐ A random thoughtful act	☐ More help	☐ Breakfast in bed	☐ Romantic dinner
☐ To feel like a million bucks	☐ Complete silence	☐ Control of remote	☐ Full-time help
☐ To look like a million bucks	☐ Extra cheese	☐ A neck rub	☐ Just a little appreciation
☐ A million bucks	☐ A bra that fits	☐ A big smile	☐ Just you

☐ **PLEASE**   ☐ **PRETTY PLEASE**   ☐ **THANK YOU**   ☐ **OR ELSE**

SIGNATURE (ACTUAL NAME OF MOTHER)   MONTH   DAY   YEAR

"IS IT REALLY SO MUCH TO ASK?"

THINGS MOM REALLY, REALLY, REALLY NEEDS

☐ **SOON** ☐ **TODAY** ☐ **RIGHT NOW** ☐ **FROM NOW ON**

SOON	TODAY	RIGHT NOW	FROM NOW ON
☐ A break	☐ For you to read my mind	☐ Candlelight	☐ Movie night
☐ Less whine	☐ An aspirin	☐ Space	☐ A side of fries
☐ More wine	☐ Some respect	☐ A well-stocked fridge	☐ Some lovin'
☐ Your love	☐ Pizza, toppings my choice	☐ Commiseration	☐ A chauffeur
☐ Chocolate	☐ A good book	☐ To sleep in	☐ Inside voices
☐ A vacation	☐ Work-life balance	☐ A margarita	☐ A little more help
☐ Peace	☐ For you to make dinner	☐ Tantrum absence	☐ Vim
☐ Quiet	☐ A little enthusiasm	☐ The toilet seat down	☐ Vigor
☐ Peace and quiet	☐ To recapture my youth	☐ Someone to take out dog	☐ A good babysitter
☐ A date night	☐ Alone time	☐ Someone to bring in cat	☐ Soft lights
☐ The toilet paper replaced	☐ Alone time in bathroom	☐ A makeover	☐ Soft music
☐ Pampering	☐ Someone to admit I'm right	☐ Costume drama on DVR	☐ Clean clothes
☐ A kiss	☐ A shopping spree	☐ Reality TV on DVR	☐ Time to read
☐ A hug	☐ Attitude of gratitude	☐ Punctuality	☐ A day without dieting
☐ A bear hug	☐ Pie	☐ Endorphin rush	☐ Calm
☐ Someone to listen	☐ A massage	☐ Personal shopper	☐ A friendly phone call
☐ Takeout	☐ An ego massage	☐ Personal schlepper	☐ A day off
☐ A little help	☐ All the answers	☐ A mate to that sock	☐ A smidgen of kindness
☐ To fit into those jeans	☐ Any answer	☐ Time to reflect	☐ A good workout
☐ Privacy	☐ Sweet nothings	☐ A little consideration	☐ A new job
☐ A love note	☐ Personal trainer	☐ Spa day	☐ Even more wine
☐ No complaints	☐ Personal assistant	☐ To be fed grapes	☐ Utter devotion
☐ Hot coffee	☐ A cup of tea	☐ A stiff one	☐ Cupcakes
☐ A hot bath	☐ Therapy	☐ Mother's little helper	☐ Thermostat control
☐ A cold shower	☐ A good night's sleep	☐ A pep talk	☐ A cold drink
☐ Some good gossip	☐ Jewelry	☐ Fewer interruptions	☐ Inner peace
☐ A day in pajamas	☐ To be the center of attention	☐ To win	☐ A day without poop
☐ A day out of sweats	☐ To sit down for a minute	☐ A sugar fix	☐ Sympathy
☐ New shoes	☐ A happy child	☐ Well-behaved inner child	☐ Empathy
☐ A bit of effort	☐ A happy spouse	☐ Well-behaved children	☐ A comfy chair
☐ Barf-free clothing	☐ Praise for my intellect	☐ To get outside	☐ Second helping of dessert
☐ Stress relief	☐ Deodorant	☐ A guilty pleasure	☐ A brisk walk
☐ Family dinner	☐ An apology	☐ A primal scream	☐ A "Please"
☐ Beds all made	☐ Lottery win	☐ A clean kitchen	☐ A "Thank you"
☐ A pick-me-up	☐ A six-pack	☐ More chocolate	☐ A present
☐ Fireman fantasy	☐ Dust bunny eradication	☐ A foot rub	☐ My prince to come
☐ The toothpaste capped	☐ A parking spot	☐ Chores completed	☐ A big bowl of ice cream
☐ A good hair day	☐ No tears	☐ Snuggle time	☐ A serenade
☐ Less laundry	☐ Stain-free day	☐ A good laugh	☐ Grace under pressure
☐ Window-shopping	☐ A haiku	☐ Clean sheets	☐ Mind over matter
☐ Complete obedience	☐ Cuddling	☐ A glass of bubbly	☐ Good will
☐ A chuckle	☐ Coddling	☐ Better neighbors	☐ Flowers
☐ Clean children	☐ A blowout	☐ To hear I'm cool	☐ A miracle
☐ A sincere compliment	☐ An empty dishwasher	☐ To hear I'm hot	☐ Some "me" time
☐ Mani-pedi	☐ You to put on a sweater	☐ Yoga	☐ A good cry
☐ A shoulder to cry on	☐ A nap	☐ Validation	☐ Girl's night out
☐ A random thoughtful act	☐ More help	☐ Breakfast in bed	☐ Romantic dinner
☐ To feel like a million bucks	☐ Complete silence	☐ Control of remote	☐ Full-time help
☐ To look like a million bucks	☐ Extra cheese	☐ A neck rub	☐ Just a little appreciation
☐ A million bucks	☐ A bra that fits	☐ A big smile	☐ Just you

☐ **PLEASE** ☐ **PRETTY PLEASE** ☐ **THANK YOU** ☐ **OR ELSE**

SIGNATURE (ACTUAL NAME OF MOTHER)

MONTH   DAY   YEAR

"IS IT REALLY SO MUCH TO ASK?"

THINGS MOM REALLY, REALLY, REALLY NEEDS

☐ **SOON**   ☐ **TODAY**   ☐ **RIGHT NOW**   ☐ **FROM NOW ON**

SOON	TODAY	RIGHT NOW	FROM NOW ON
☐ A break	☐ For you to read my mind	☐ Candlelight	☐ Movie night
☐ Less whine	☐ An aspirin	☐ Space	☐ A side of fries
☐ More wine	☐ Some respect	☐ A well-stocked fridge	☐ Some lovin'
☐ Your love	☐ Pizza, toppings my choice	☐ Commiseration	☐ A chauffeur
☐ Chocolate	☐ A good book	☐ To sleep in	☐ Inside voices
☐ A vacation	☐ Work-life balance	☐ A margarita	☐ A little more help
☐ Peace	☐ For you to make dinner	☐ Tantrum absence	☐ Vim
☐ Quiet	☐ A little enthusiasm	☐ The toilet seat down	☐ Vigor
☐ Peace and quiet	☐ To recapture my youth	☐ Someone to take out dog	☐ A good babysitter
☐ A date night	☐ Alone time	☐ Someone to bring in cat	☐ Soft lights
☐ The toilet paper replaced	☐ Alone time in bathroom	☐ A makeover	☐ Soft music
☐ Pampering	☐ Someone to admit I'm right	☐ Costume drama on DVR	☐ Clean clothes
☐ A kiss	☐ A shopping spree	☐ Reality TV on DVR	☐ Time to read
☐ A hug	☐ Attitude of gratitude	☐ Punctuality	☐ A day without dieting
☐ A bear hug	☐ Pie	☐ Endorphin rush	☐ Calm
☐ Someone to listen	☐ A massage	☐ Personal shopper	☐ A friendly phone call
☐ Takeout	☐ An ego massage	☐ Personal schlepper	☐ A day off
☐ A little help	☐ All the answers	☐ A mate to that sock	☐ A smidgen of kindness
☐ To fit into those jeans	☐ Any answer	☐ Time to reflect	☐ A good workout
☐ Privacy	☐ Sweet nothings	☐ A little consideration	☐ A new job
☐ A love note	☐ Personal trainer	☐ Spa day	☐ Even more wine
☐ No complaints	☐ Personal assistant	☐ To be fed grapes	☐ Utter devotion
☐ Hot coffee	☐ A cup of tea	☐ A stiff one	☐ Cupcakes
☐ A hot bath	☐ Therapy	☐ Mother's little helper	☐ Thermostat control
☐ A cold shower	☐ A good night's sleep	☐ A pep talk	☐ A cold drink
☐ Some good gossip	☐ Jewelry	☐ Fewer interruptions	☐ Inner peace
☐ A day in pajamas	☐ To be the center of attention	☐ To win	☐ A day without poop
☐ A day out of sweats	☐ To sit down for a minute	☐ A sugar fix	☐ Sympathy
☐ New shoes	☐ A happy child	☐ Well-behaved inner child	☐ Empathy
☐ A bit of effort	☐ A happy spouse	☐ Well-behaved children	☐ A comfy chair
☐ Barf-free clothing	☐ Praise for my intellect	☐ To get outside	☐ Second helping of dessert
☐ Stress relief	☐ Deodorant	☐ A guilty pleasure	☐ A brisk walk
☐ Family dinner	☐ An apology	☐ A primal scream	☐ A "Please"
☐ Beds all made	☐ Lottery win	☐ A clean kitchen	☐ A "Thank you"
☐ A pick-me-up	☐ A six-pack	☐ More chocolate	☐ A present
☐ Fireman fantasy	☐ Dust bunny eradication	☐ A foot rub	☐ My prince to come
☐ The toothpaste capped	☐ A parking spot	☐ Chores completed	☐ A big bowl of ice cream
☐ A good hair day	☐ No tears	☐ Snuggle time	☐ A serenade
☐ Less laundry	☐ Stain-free day	☐ A good laugh	☐ Grace under pressure
☐ Window-shopping	☐ A haiku	☐ Clean sheets	☐ Mind over matter
☐ Complete obedience	☐ Cuddling	☐ A glass of bubbly	☐ Good will
☐ A chuckle	☐ Coddling	☐ Better neighbors	☐ Flowers
☐ Clean children	☐ A blowout	☐ To hear I'm cool	☐ A miracle
☐ A sincere compliment	☐ An empty dishwasher	☐ To hear I'm hot	☐ Some "me" time
☐ Mani-pedi	☐ You to put on a sweater	☐ Yoga	☐ A good cry
☐ A shoulder to cry on	☐ A nap	☐ Validation	☐ Girl's night out
☐ A random thoughtful act	☐ More help	☐ Breakfast in bed	☐ Romantic dinner
☐ To feel like a million bucks	☐ Complete silence	☐ Control of remote	☐ Full-time help
☐ To look like a million bucks	☐ Extra cheese	☐ A neck rub	☐ Just a little appreciation
☐ A million bucks	☐ A bra that fits	☐ A big smile	☐ Just you

☐ **PLEASE**   ☐ **PRETTY PLEASE**   ☐ **THANK YOU**   ☐ **OR ELSE**

SIGNATURE (ACTUAL NAME OF MOTHER) | MONTH | DAY | YEAR

"IS IT REALLY SO MUCH TO ASK?"

THINGS MOM REALLY, REALLY, REALLY NEEDS

☐ **SOON**　　☐ **TODAY**　　☐ **RIGHT NOW**　　☐ **FROM NOW ON**

☐ A break	☐ For you to read my mind	☐ Candlelight	☐ Movie night
☐ Less whine	☐ An aspirin	☐ Space	☐ A side of fries
☐ More wine	☐ Some respect	☐ A well-stocked fridge	☐ Some lovin'
☐ Your love	☐ Pizza, toppings my choice	☐ Commiseration	☐ A chauffeur
☐ Chocolate	☐ A good book	☐ To sleep in	☐ Inside voices
☐ A vacation	☐ Work-life balance	☐ A margarita	☐ A little more help
☐ Peace	☐ For you to make dinner	☐ Tantrum absence	☐ Vim
☐ Quiet	☐ A little enthusiasm	☐ The toilet seat down	☐ Vigor
☐ Peace and quiet	☐ To recapture my youth	☐ Someone to take out dog	☐ A good babysitter
☐ A date night	☐ Alone time	☐ Someone to bring in cat	☐ Soft lights
☐ The toilet paper replaced	☐ Alone time in bathroom	☐ A makeover	☐ Soft music
☐ Pampering	☐ Someone to admit I'm right	☐ Costume drama on DVR	☐ Clean clothes
☐ A kiss	☐ A shopping spree	☐ Reality TV on DVR	☐ Time to read
☐ A hug	☐ Attitude of gratitude	☐ Punctuality	☐ A day without dieting
☐ A bear hug	☐ Pie	☐ Endorphin rush	☐ Calm
☐ Someone to listen	☐ A massage	☐ Personal shopper	☐ A friendly phone call
☐ Takeout	☐ An ego massage	☐ Personal schlepper	☐ A day off
☐ A little help	☐ All the answers	☐ A mate to that sock	☐ A smidgen of kindness
☐ To fit into those jeans	☐ Any answer	☐ Time to reflect	☐ A good workout
☐ Privacy	☐ Sweet nothings	☐ A little consideration	☐ A new job
☐ A love note	☐ Personal trainer	☐ Spa day	☐ Even more wine
☐ No complaints	☐ Personal assistant	☐ To be fed grapes	☐ Utter devotion
☐ Hot coffee	☐ A cup of tea	☐ A stiff one	☐ Cupcakes
☐ A hot bath	☐ Therapy	☐ Mother's little helper	☐ Thermostat control
☐ A cold shower	☐ A good night's sleep	☐ A pep talk	☐ A cold drink
☐ Some good gossip	☐ Jewelry	☐ Fewer interruptions	☐ Inner peace
☐ A day in pajamas	☐ To be the center of attention	☐ To win	☐ A day without poop
☐ A day out of sweats	☐ To sit down for a minute	☐ A sugar fix	☐ Sympathy
☐ New shoes	☐ A happy child	☐ Well-behaved inner child	☐ Empathy
☐ A bit of effort	☐ A happy spouse	☐ Well-behaved children	☐ A comfy chair
☐ Barf-free clothing	☐ Praise for my intellect	☐ To get outside	☐ Second helping of dessert
☐ Stress relief	☐ Deodorant	☐ A guilty pleasure	☐ A brisk walk
☐ Family dinner	☐ An apology	☐ A primal scream	☐ A "Please"
☐ Beds all made	☐ Lottery win	☐ A clean kitchen	☐ A "Thank you"
☐ A pick-me-up	☐ A six-pack	☐ More chocolate	☐ A present
☐ Fireman fantasy	☐ Dust bunny eradication	☐ A foot rub	☐ My prince to come
☐ The toothpaste capped	☐ A parking spot	☐ Chores completed	☐ A big bowl of ice cream
☐ A good hair day	☐ No tears	☐ Snuggle time	☐ A serenade
☐ Less laundry	☐ Stain-free day	☐ A good laugh	☐ Grace under pressure
☐ Window-shopping	☐ A haiku	☐ Clean sheets	☐ Mind over matter
☐ Complete obedience	☐ Cuddling	☐ A glass of bubbly	☐ Good will
☐ A chuckle	☐ Coddling	☐ Better neighbors	☐ Flowers
☐ Clean children	☐ A blowout	☐ To hear I'm cool	☐ A miracle
☐ A sincere compliment	☐ An empty dishwasher	☐ To hear I'm hot	☐ Some "me" time
☐ Mani-pedi	☐ You to put on a sweater	☐ Yoga	☐ A good cry
☐ A shoulder to cry on	☐ A nap	☐ Validation	☐ Girl's night out
☐ A random thoughtful act	☐ More help	☐ Breakfast in bed	☐ Romantic dinner
☐ To feel like a million bucks	☐ Complete silence	☐ Control of remote	☐ Full-time help
☐ To look like a million bucks	☐ Extra cheese	☐ A neck rub	☐ Just a little appreciation
☐ A million bucks	☐ A bra that fits	☐ A big smile	☐ Just you

☐ **PLEASE**　　☐ **PRETTY PLEASE**　　☐ **THANK YOU**　　☐ **OR ELSE**

SIGNATURE (ACTUAL NAME OF MOTHER)　　MONTH ┆ DAY ┆ YEAR

"IS IT REALLY SO MUCH TO ASK?"

THINGS MOM REALLY, REALLY, REALLY NEEDS

☐ **SOON**　　☐ **TODAY**　　☐ **RIGHT NOW**　　☐ **FROM NOW ON**

☐ A break	☐ For you to read my mind	☐ Candlelight	☐ Movie night
☐ Less whine	☐ An aspirin	☐ Space	☐ A side of fries
☐ More wine	☐ Some respect	☐ A well-stocked fridge	☐ Some lovin'
☐ Your love	☐ Pizza, toppings my choice	☐ Commiseration	☐ A chauffeur
☐ Chocolate	☐ A good book	☐ To sleep in	☐ Inside voices
☐ A vacation	☐ Work-life balance	☐ A margarita	☐ A little more help
☐ Peace	☐ For you to make dinner	☐ Tantrum absence	☐ Vim
☐ Quiet	☐ A little enthusiasm	☐ The toilet seat down	☐ Vigor
☐ Peace and quiet	☐ To recapture my youth	☐ Someone to take out dog	☐ A good babysitter
☐ A date night	☐ Alone time	☐ Someone to bring in cat	☐ Soft lights
☐ The toilet paper replaced	☐ Alone time in bathroom	☐ A makeover	☐ Soft music
☐ Pampering	☐ Someone to admit I'm right	☐ Costume drama on DVR	☐ Clean clothes
☐ A kiss	☐ A shopping spree	☐ Reality TV on DVR	☐ Time to read
☐ A hug	☐ Attitude of gratitude	☐ Punctuality	☐ A day without dieting
☐ A bear hug	☐ Pie	☐ Endorphin rush	☐ Calm
☐ Someone to listen	☐ A massage	☐ Personal shopper	☐ A friendly phone call
☐ Takeout	☐ An ego massage	☐ Personal schlepper	☐ A day off
☐ A little help	☐ All the answers	☐ A mate to that sock	☐ A smidgen of kindness
☐ To fit into those jeans	☐ Any answer	☐ Time to reflect	☐ A good workout
☐ Privacy	☐ Sweet nothings	☐ A little consideration	☐ A new job
☐ A love note	☐ Personal trainer	☐ Spa day	☐ Even more wine
☐ No complaints	☐ Personal assistant	☐ To be fed grapes	☐ Utter devotion
☐ Hot coffee	☐ A cup of tea	☐ A stiff one	☐ Cupcakes
☐ A hot bath	☐ Therapy	☐ Mother's little helper	☐ Thermostat control
☐ A cold shower	☐ A good night's sleep	☐ A pep talk	☐ A cold drink
☐ Some good gossip	☐ Jewelry	☐ Fewer interruptions	☐ Inner peace
☐ A day in pajamas	☐ To be the center of attention	☐ To win	☐ A day without poop
☐ A day out of sweats	☐ To sit down for a minute	☐ A sugar fix	☐ Sympathy
☐ New shoes	☐ A happy child	☐ Well-behaved inner child	☐ Empathy
☐ A bit of effort	☐ A happy spouse	☐ Well-behaved children	☐ A comfy chair
☐ Barf-free clothing	☐ Praise for my intellect	☐ To get outside	☐ Second helping of dessert
☐ Stress relief	☐ Deodorant	☐ A guilty pleasure	☐ A brisk walk
☐ Family dinner	☐ An apology	☐ A primal scream	☐ A "Please"
☐ Beds all made	☐ Lottery win	☐ A clean kitchen	☐ A "Thank you"
☐ A pick-me-up	☐ A six-pack	☐ More chocolate	☐ A present
☐ Fireman fantasy	☐ Dust bunny eradication	☐ A foot rub	☐ My prince to come
☐ The toothpaste capped	☐ A parking spot	☐ Chores completed	☐ A big bowl of ice cream
☐ A good hair day	☐ No tears	☐ Snuggle time	☐ A serenade
☐ Less laundry	☐ Stain-free day	☐ A good laugh	☐ Grace under pressure
☐ Window-shopping	☐ A haiku	☐ Clean sheets	☐ Mind over matter
☐ Complete obedience	☐ Cuddling	☐ A glass of bubbly	☐ Good will
☐ A chuckle	☐ Coddling	☐ Better neighbors	☐ Flowers
☐ Clean children	☐ A blowout	☐ To hear I'm cool	☐ A miracle
☐ A sincere compliment	☐ An empty dishwasher	☐ To hear I'm hot	☐ Some "me" time
☐ Mani-pedi	☐ You to put on a sweater	☐ Yoga	☐ A good cry
☐ A shoulder to cry on	☐ A nap	☐ Validation	☐ Girl's night out
☐ A random thoughtful act	☐ More help	☐ Breakfast in bed	☐ Romantic dinner
☐ To feel like a million bucks	☐ Complete silence	☐ Control of remote	☐ Full-time help
☐ To look like a million bucks	☐ Extra cheese	☐ A neck rub	☐ Just a little appreciation
☐ A million bucks	☐ A bra that fits	☐ A big smile	☐ Just you

☐ **PLEASE**　　☐ **PRETTY PLEASE**　　☐ **THANK YOU**　　☐ **OR ELSE**

SIGNATURE (ACTUAL NAME OF MOTHER)　　MONTH　DAY　YEAR

"IS IT REALLY SO MUCH TO ASK?"

THINGS MOM REALLY, REALLY, REALLY NEEDS

☐ **SOON**   ☐ **TODAY**   ☐ **RIGHT NOW**   ☐ **FROM NOW ON**

SOON	TODAY	RIGHT NOW	FROM NOW ON
☐ A break	☐ For you to read my mind	☐ Candlelight	☐ Movie night
☐ Less whine	☐ An aspirin	☐ Space	☐ A side of fries
☐ More wine	☐ Some respect	☐ A well-stocked fridge	☐ Some lovin'
☐ Your love	☐ Pizza, toppings my choice	☐ Commiseration	☐ A chauffeur
☐ Chocolate	☐ A good book	☐ To sleep in	☐ Inside voices
☐ A vacation	☐ Work-life balance	☐ A margarita	☐ A little more help
☐ Peace	☐ For you to make dinner	☐ Tantrum absence	☐ Vim
☐ Quiet	☐ A little enthusiasm	☐ The toilet seat down	☐ Vigor
☐ Peace and quiet	☐ To recapture my youth	☐ Someone to take out dog	☐ A good babysitter
☐ A date night	☐ Alone time	☐ Someone to bring in cat	☐ Soft lights
☐ The toilet paper replaced	☐ Alone time in bathroom	☐ A makeover	☐ Soft music
☐ Pampering	☐ Someone to admit I'm right	☐ Costume drama on DVR	☐ Clean clothes
☐ A kiss	☐ A shopping spree	☐ Reality TV on DVR	☐ Time to read
☐ A hug	☐ Attitude of gratitude	☐ Punctuality	☐ A day without dieting
☐ A bear hug	☐ Pie	☐ Endorphin rush	☐ Calm
☐ Someone to listen	☐ A massage	☐ Personal shopper	☐ A friendly phone call
☐ Takeout	☐ An ego massage	☐ Personal schlepper	☐ A day off
☐ A little help	☐ All the answers	☐ A mate to that sock	☐ A smidgen of kindness
☐ To fit into those jeans	☐ Any answer	☐ Time to reflect	☐ A good workout
☐ Privacy	☐ Sweet nothings	☐ A little consideration	☐ A new job
☐ A love note	☐ Personal trainer	☐ Spa day	☐ Even more wine
☐ No complaints	☐ Personal assistant	☐ To be fed grapes	☐ Utter devotion
☐ Hot coffee	☐ A cup of tea	☐ A stiff one	☐ Cupcakes
☐ A hot bath	☐ Therapy	☐ Mother's little helper	☐ Thermostat control
☐ A cold shower	☐ A good night's sleep	☐ A pep talk	☐ A cold drink
☐ Some good gossip	☐ Jewelry	☐ Fewer interruptions	☐ Inner peace
☐ A day in pajamas	☐ To be the center of attention	☐ To win	☐ A day without poop
☐ A day out of sweats	☐ To sit down for a minute	☐ A sugar fix	☐ Sympathy
☐ New shoes	☐ A happy child	☐ Well-behaved inner child	☐ Empathy
☐ A bit of effort	☐ A happy spouse	☐ Well-behaved children	☐ A comfy chair
☐ Barf-free clothing	☐ Praise for my intellect	☐ To get outside	☐ Second helping of dessert
☐ Stress relief	☐ Deodorant	☐ A guilty pleasure	☐ A brisk walk
☐ Family dinner	☐ An apology	☐ A primal scream	☐ A "Please"
☐ Beds all made	☐ Lottery win	☐ A clean kitchen	☐ A "Thank you"
☐ A pick-me-up	☐ A six-pack	☐ More chocolate	☐ A present
☐ Fireman fantasy	☐ Dust bunny eradication	☐ A foot rub	☐ My prince to come
☐ The toothpaste capped	☐ A parking spot	☐ Chores completed	☐ A big bowl of ice cream
☐ A good hair day	☐ No tears	☐ Snuggle time	☐ A serenade
☐ Less laundry	☐ Stain-free day	☐ A good laugh	☐ Grace under pressure
☐ Window-shopping	☐ A haiku	☐ Clean sheets	☐ Mind over matter
☐ Complete obedience	☐ Cuddling	☐ A glass of bubbly	☐ Good will
☐ A chuckle	☐ Coddling	☐ Better neighbors	☐ Flowers
☐ Clean children	☐ A blowout	☐ To hear I'm cool	☐ A miracle
☐ A sincere compliment	☐ An empty dishwasher	☐ To hear I'm hot	☐ Some "me" time
☐ Mani-pedi	☐ You to put on a sweater	☐ Yoga	☐ A good cry
☐ A shoulder to cry on	☐ A nap	☐ Validation	☐ Girl's night out
☐ A random thoughtful act	☐ More help	☐ Breakfast in bed	☐ Romantic dinner
☐ To feel like a million bucks	☐ Complete silence	☐ Control of remote	☐ Full-time help
☐ To look like a million bucks	☐ Extra cheese	☐ A neck rub	☐ Just a little appreciation
☐ A million bucks	☐ A bra that fits	☐ A big smile	☐ Just you

☐ **PLEASE**   ☐ **PRETTY PLEASE**   ☐ **THANK YOU**   ☐ **OR ELSE**

SIGNATURE (ACTUAL NAME OF MOTHER)	MONTH	DAY	YEAR

"IS IT REALLY SO MUCH TO ASK?"

THINGS MOM REALLY, REALLY, REALLY NEEDS

☐ **SOON**   ☐ **TODAY**   ☐ **RIGHT NOW**   ☐ **FROM NOW ON**

☐ A break	☐ For you to read my mind	☐ Candlelight	☐ Movie night
☐ Less whine	☐ An aspirin	☐ Space	☐ A side of fries
☐ More wine	☐ Some respect	☐ A well-stocked fridge	☐ Some lovin'
☐ Your love	☐ Pizza, toppings my choice	☐ Commiseration	☐ A chauffeur
☐ Chocolate	☐ A good book	☐ To sleep in	☐ Inside voices
☐ A vacation	☐ Work-life balance	☐ A margarita	☐ A little more help
☐ Peace	☐ For you to make dinner	☐ Tantrum absence	☐ Vim
☐ Quiet	☐ A little enthusiasm	☐ The toilet seat down	☐ Vigor
☐ Peace and quiet	☐ To recapture my youth	☐ Someone to take out dog	☐ A good babysitter
☐ A date night	☐ Alone time	☐ Someone to bring in cat	☐ Soft lights
☐ The toilet paper replaced	☐ Alone time in bathroom	☐ A makeover	☐ Soft music
☐ Pampering	☐ Someone to admit I'm right	☐ Costume drama on DVR	☐ Clean clothes
☐ A kiss	☐ A shopping spree	☐ Reality TV on DVR	☐ Time to read
☐ A hug	☐ Attitude of gratitude	☐ Punctuality	☐ A day without dieting
☐ A bear hug	☐ Pie	☐ Endorphin rush	☐ Calm
☐ Someone to listen	☐ A massage	☐ Personal shopper	☐ A friendly phone call
☐ Takeout	☐ An ego massage	☐ Personal schlepper	☐ A day off
☐ A little help	☐ All the answers	☐ A mate to that sock	☐ A smidgen of kindness
☐ To fit into those jeans	☐ Any answer	☐ Time to reflect	☐ A good workout
☐ Privacy	☐ Sweet nothings	☐ A little consideration	☐ A new job
☐ A love note	☐ Personal trainer	☐ Spa day	☐ Even more wine
☐ No complaints	☐ Personal assistant	☐ To be fed grapes	☐ Utter devotion
☐ Hot coffee	☐ A cup of tea	☐ A stiff one	☐ Cupcakes
☐ A hot bath	☐ Therapy	☐ Mother's little helper	☐ Thermostat control
☐ A cold shower	☐ A good night's sleep	☐ A pep talk	☐ A cold drink
☐ Some good gossip	☐ Jewelry	☐ Fewer interruptions	☐ Inner peace
☐ A day in pajamas	☐ To be the center of attention	☐ To win	☐ A day without poop
☐ A day out of sweats	☐ To sit down for a minute	☐ A sugar fix	☐ Sympathy
☐ New shoes	☐ A happy child	☐ Well-behaved inner child	☐ Empathy
☐ A bit of effort	☐ A happy spouse	☐ Well-behaved children	☐ A comfy chair
☐ Barf-free clothing	☐ Praise for my intellect	☐ To get outside	☐ Second helping of dessert
☐ Stress relief	☐ Deodorant	☐ A guilty pleasure	☐ A brisk walk
☐ Family dinner	☐ An apology	☐ A primal scream	☐ A "Please"
☐ Beds all made	☐ Lottery win	☐ A clean kitchen	☐ A "Thank you"
☐ A pick-me-up	☐ A six-pack	☐ More chocolate	☐ A present
☐ Fireman fantasy	☐ Dust bunny eradication	☐ A foot rub	☐ My prince to come
☐ The toothpaste capped	☐ A parking spot	☐ Chores completed	☐ A big bowl of ice cream
☐ A good hair day	☐ No tears	☐ Snuggle time	☐ A serenade
☐ Less laundry	☐ Stain-free day	☐ A good laugh	☐ Grace under pressure
☐ Window-shopping	☐ A haiku	☐ Clean sheets	☐ Mind over matter
☐ Complete obedience	☐ Cuddling	☐ A glass of bubbly	☐ Good will
☐ A chuckle	☐ Coddling	☐ Better neighbors	☐ Flowers
☐ Clean children	☐ A blowout	☐ To hear I'm cool	☐ A miracle
☐ A sincere compliment	☐ An empty dishwasher	☐ To hear I'm hot	☐ Some "me" time
☐ Mani-pedi	☐ You to put on a sweater	☐ Yoga	☐ A good cry
☐ A shoulder to cry on	☐ A nap	☐ Validation	☐ Girl's night out
☐ A random thoughtful act	☐ More help	☐ Breakfast in bed	☐ Romantic dinner
☐ To feel like a million bucks	☐ Complete silence	☐ Control of remote	☐ Full-time help
☐ To look like a million bucks	☐ Extra cheese	☐ A neck rub	☐ Just a little appreciation
☐ A million bucks	☐ A bra that fits	☐ A big smile	☐ Just you

☐ **PLEASE**   ☐ **PRETTY PLEASE**   ☐ **THANK YOU**   ☐ **OR ELSE**

SIGNATURE (ACTUAL NAME OF MOTHER)   MONTH   DAY   YEAR

"IS IT REALLY SO MUCH TO ASK?"

THINGS MOM REALLY, REALLY, REALLY NEEDS

☐ **SOON** ☐ **TODAY** ☐ **RIGHT NOW** ☐ **FROM NOW ON**

SOON	TODAY	RIGHT NOW	FROM NOW ON
☐ A break	☐ For you to read my mind	☐ Candlelight	☐ Movie night
☐ Less whine	☐ An aspirin	☐ Space	☐ A side of fries
☐ More wine	☐ Some respect	☐ A well-stocked fridge	☐ Some lovin'
☐ Your love	☐ Pizza, toppings my choice	☐ Commiseration	☐ A chauffeur
☐ Chocolate	☐ A good book	☐ To sleep in	☐ Inside voices
☐ A vacation	☐ Work-life balance	☐ A margarita	☐ A little more help
☐ Peace	☐ For you to make dinner	☐ Tantrum absence	☐ Vim
☐ Quiet	☐ A little enthusiasm	☐ The toilet seat down	☐ Vigor
☐ Peace and quiet	☐ To recapture my youth	☐ Someone to take out dog	☐ A good babysitter
☐ A date night	☐ Alone time	☐ Someone to bring in cat	☐ Soft lights
☐ The toilet paper replaced	☐ Alone time in bathroom	☐ A makeover	☐ Soft music
☐ Pampering	☐ Someone to admit I'm right	☐ Costume drama on DVR	☐ Clean clothes
☐ A kiss	☐ A shopping spree	☐ Reality TV on DVR	☐ Time to read
☐ A hug	☐ Attitude of gratitude	☐ Punctuality	☐ A day without dieting
☐ A bear hug	☐ Pie	☐ Endorphin rush	☐ Calm
☐ Someone to listen	☐ A massage	☐ Personal shopper	☐ A friendly phone call
☐ Takeout	☐ An ego massage	☐ Personal schlepper	☐ A day off
☐ A little help	☐ All the answers	☐ A mate to that sock	☐ A smidgen of kindness
☐ To fit into those jeans	☐ Any answer	☐ Time to reflect	☐ A good workout
☐ Privacy	☐ Sweet nothings	☐ A little consideration	☐ A new job
☐ A love note	☐ Personal trainer	☐ Spa day	☐ Even more wine
☐ No complaints	☐ Personal assistant	☐ To be fed grapes	☐ Utter devotion
☐ Hot coffee	☐ A cup of tea	☐ A stiff one	☐ Cupcakes
☐ A hot bath	☐ Therapy	☐ Mother's little helper	☐ Thermostat control
☐ A cold shower	☐ A good night's sleep	☐ A pep talk	☐ A cold drink
☐ Some good gossip	☐ Jewelry	☐ Fewer interruptions	☐ Inner peace
☐ A day in pajamas	☐ To be the center of attention	☐ To win	☐ A day without poop
☐ A day out of sweats	☐ To sit down for a minute	☐ A sugar fix	☐ Sympathy
☐ New shoes	☐ A happy child	☐ Well-behaved inner child	☐ Empathy
☐ A bit of effort	☐ A happy spouse	☐ Well-behaved children	☐ A comfy chair
☐ Barf-free clothing	☐ Praise for my intellect	☐ To get outside	☐ Second helping of dessert
☐ Stress relief	☐ Deodorant	☐ A guilty pleasure	☐ A brisk walk
☐ Family dinner	☐ An apology	☐ A primal scream	☐ A "Please"
☐ Beds all made	☐ Lottery win	☐ A clean kitchen	☐ A "Thank you"
☐ A pick-me-up	☐ A six-pack	☐ More chocolate	☐ A present
☐ Fireman fantasy	☐ Dust bunny eradication	☐ A foot rub	☐ My prince to come
☐ The toothpaste capped	☐ A parking spot	☐ Chores completed	☐ A big bowl of ice cream
☐ A good hair day	☐ No tears	☐ Snuggle time	☐ A serenade
☐ Less laundry	☐ Stain-free day	☐ A good laugh	☐ Grace under pressure
☐ Window-shopping	☐ A haiku	☐ Clean sheets	☐ Mind over matter
☐ Complete obedience	☐ Cuddling	☐ A glass of bubbly	☐ Good will
☐ A chuckle	☐ Coddling	☐ Better neighbors	☐ Flowers
☐ Clean children	☐ A blowout	☐ To hear I'm cool	☐ A miracle
☐ A sincere compliment	☐ An empty dishwasher	☐ To hear I'm hot	☐ Some "me" time
☐ Mani-pedi	☐ You to put on a sweater	☐ Yoga	☐ A good cry
☐ A shoulder to cry on	☐ A nap	☐ Validation	☐ Girl's night out
☐ A random thoughtful act	☐ More help	☐ Breakfast in bed	☐ Romantic dinner
☐ To feel like a million bucks	☐ Complete silence	☐ Control of remote	☐ Full-time help
☐ To look like a million bucks	☐ Extra cheese	☐ A neck rub	☐ Just a little appreciation
☐ A million bucks	☐ A bra that fits	☐ A big smile	☐ Just you

☐ **PLEASE** ☐ **PRETTY PLEASE** ☐ **THANK YOU** ☐ **OR ELSE**

SIGNATURE (ACTUAL NAME OF MOTHER) MONTH DAY YEAR

"IS IT REALLY SO MUCH TO ASK?"

THINGS MOM REALLY, REALLY, REALLY NEEDS

☐ **SOON** ☐ **TODAY** ☐ **RIGHT NOW** ☐ **FROM NOW ON**

SOON	TODAY	RIGHT NOW	FROM NOW ON
☐ A break	☐ For you to read my mind	☐ Candlelight	☐ Movie night
☐ Less whine	☐ An aspirin	☐ Space	☐ A side of fries
☐ More wine	☐ Some respect	☐ A well-stocked fridge	☐ Some lovin'
☐ Your love	☐ Pizza, toppings my choice	☐ Commiseration	☐ A chauffeur
☐ Chocolate	☐ A good book	☐ To sleep in	☐ Inside voices
☐ A vacation	☐ Work-life balance	☐ A margarita	☐ A little more help
☐ Peace	☐ For you to make dinner	☐ Tantrum absence	☐ Vim
☐ Quiet	☐ A little enthusiasm	☐ The toilet seat down	☐ Vigor
☐ Peace and quiet	☐ To recapture my youth	☐ Someone to take out dog	☐ A good babysitter
☐ A date night	☐ Alone time	☐ Someone to bring in cat	☐ Soft lights
☐ The toilet paper replaced	☐ Alone time in bathroom	☐ A makeover	☐ Soft music
☐ Pampering	☐ Someone to admit I'm right	☐ Costume drama on DVR	☐ Clean clothes
☐ A kiss	☐ A shopping spree	☐ Reality TV on DVR	☐ Time to read
☐ A hug	☐ Attitude of gratitude	☐ Punctuality	☐ A day without dieting
☐ A bear hug	☐ Pie	☐ Endorphin rush	☐ Calm
☐ Someone to listen	☐ A massage	☐ Personal shopper	☐ A friendly phone call
☐ Takeout	☐ An ego massage	☐ Personal schlepper	☐ A day off
☐ A little help	☐ All the answers	☐ A mate to that sock	☐ A smidgen of kindness
☐ To fit into those jeans	☐ Any answer	☐ Time to reflect	☐ A good workout
☐ Privacy	☐ Sweet nothings	☐ A little consideration	☐ A new job
☐ A love note	☐ Personal trainer	☐ Spa day	☐ Even more wine
☐ No complaints	☐ Personal assistant	☐ To be fed grapes	☐ Utter devotion
☐ Hot coffee	☐ A cup of tea	☐ A stiff one	☐ Cupcakes
☐ A hot bath	☐ Therapy	☐ Mother's little helper	☐ Thermostat control
☐ A cold shower	☐ A good night's sleep	☐ A pep talk	☐ A cold drink
☐ Some good gossip	☐ Jewelry	☐ Fewer interruptions	☐ Inner peace
☐ A day in pajamas	☐ To be the center of attention	☐ To win	☐ A day without poop
☐ A day out of sweats	☐ To sit down for a minute	☐ A sugar fix	☐ Sympathy
☐ New shoes	☐ A happy child	☐ Well-behaved inner child	☐ Empathy
☐ A bit of effort	☐ A happy spouse	☐ Well-behaved children	☐ A comfy chair
☐ Barf-free clothing	☐ Praise for my intellect	☐ To get outside	☐ Second helping of dessert
☐ Stress relief	☐ Deodorant	☐ A guilty pleasure	☐ A brisk walk
☐ Family dinner	☐ An apology	☐ A primal scream	☐ A "Please"
☐ Beds all made	☐ Lottery win	☐ A clean kitchen	☐ A "Thank you"
☐ A pick-me-up	☐ A six-pack	☐ More chocolate	☐ A present
☐ Fireman fantasy	☐ Dust bunny eradication	☐ A foot rub	☐ My prince to come
☐ The toothpaste capped	☐ A parking spot	☐ Chores completed	☐ A big bowl of ice cream
☐ A good hair day	☐ No tears	☐ Snuggle time	☐ A serenade
☐ Less laundry	☐ Stain-free day	☐ A good laugh	☐ Grace under pressure
☐ Window-shopping	☐ A haiku	☐ Clean sheets	☐ Mind over matter
☐ Complete obedience	☐ Cuddling	☐ A glass of bubbly	☐ Good will
☐ A chuckle	☐ Coddling	☐ Better neighbors	☐ Flowers
☐ Clean children	☐ A blowout	☐ To hear I'm cool	☐ A miracle
☐ A sincere compliment	☐ An empty dishwasher	☐ To hear I'm hot	☐ Some "me" time
☐ Mani-pedi	☐ You to put on a sweater	☐ Yoga	☐ A good cry
☐ A shoulder to cry on	☐ A nap	☐ Validation	☐ Girl's night out
☐ A random thoughtful act	☐ More help	☐ Breakfast in bed	☐ Romantic dinner
☐ To feel like a million bucks	☐ Complete silence	☐ Control of remote	☐ Full-time help
☐ To look like a million bucks	☐ Extra cheese	☐ A neck rub	☐ Just a little appreciation
☐ A million bucks	☐ A bra that fits	☐ A big smile	☐ Just you

☐ **PLEASE** ☐ **PRETTY PLEASE** ☐ **THANK YOU** ☐ **OR ELSE**

SIGNATURE (ACTUAL NAME OF MOTHER)   MONTH   DAY   YEAR

"IS IT REALLY SO MUCH TO ASK?"

THINGS MOM REALLY, REALLY, REALLY NEEDS

☐ **SOON**   ☐ **TODAY**   ☐ **RIGHT NOW**   ☐ **FROM NOW ON**

SOON	TODAY	RIGHT NOW	FROM NOW ON
☐ A break	☐ For you to read my mind	☐ Candlelight	☐ Movie night
☐ Less whine	☐ An aspirin	☐ Space	☐ A side of fries
☐ More wine	☐ Some respect	☐ A well-stocked fridge	☐ Some lovin'
☐ Your love	☐ Pizza, toppings my choice	☐ Commiseration	☐ A chauffeur
☐ Chocolate	☐ A good book	☐ To sleep in	☐ Inside voices
☐ A vacation	☐ Work-life balance	☐ A margarita	☐ A little more help
☐ Peace	☐ For you to make dinner	☐ Tantrum absence	☐ Vim
☐ Quiet	☐ A little enthusiasm	☐ The toilet seat down	☐ Vigor
☐ Peace and quiet	☐ To recapture my youth	☐ Someone to take out dog	☐ A good babysitter
☐ A date night	☐ Alone time	☐ Someone to bring in cat	☐ Soft lights
☐ The toilet paper replaced	☐ Alone time in bathroom	☐ A makeover	☐ Soft music
☐ Pampering	☐ Someone to admit I'm right	☐ Costume drama on DVR	☐ Clean clothes
☐ A kiss	☐ A shopping spree	☐ Reality TV on DVR	☐ Time to read
☐ A hug	☐ Attitude of gratitude	☐ Punctuality	☐ A day without dieting
☐ A bear hug	☐ Pie	☐ Endorphin rush	☐ Calm
☐ Someone to listen	☐ A massage	☐ Personal shopper	☐ A friendly phone call
☐ Takeout	☐ An ego massage	☐ Personal schlepper	☐ A day off
☐ A little help	☐ All the answers	☐ A mate to that sock	☐ A smidgen of kindness
☐ To fit into those jeans	☐ Any answer	☐ Time to reflect	☐ A good workout
☐ Privacy	☐ Sweet nothings	☐ A little consideration	☐ A new job
☐ A love note	☐ Personal trainer	☐ Spa day	☐ Even more wine
☐ No complaints	☐ Personal assistant	☐ To be fed grapes	☐ Utter devotion
☐ Hot coffee	☐ A cup of tea	☐ A stiff one	☐ Cupcakes
☐ A hot bath	☐ Therapy	☐ Mother's little helper	☐ Thermostat control
☐ A cold shower	☐ A good night's sleep	☐ A pep talk	☐ A cold drink
☐ Some good gossip	☐ Jewelry	☐ Fewer interruptions	☐ Inner peace
☐ A day in pajamas	☐ To be the center of attention	☐ To win	☐ A day without poop
☐ A day out of sweats	☐ To sit down for a minute	☐ A sugar fix	☐ Sympathy
☐ New shoes	☐ A happy child	☐ Well-behaved inner child	☐ Empathy
☐ A bit of effort	☐ A happy spouse	☐ Well-behaved children	☐ A comfy chair
☐ Barf-free clothing	☐ Praise for my intellect	☐ To get outside	☐ Second helping of dessert
☐ Stress relief	☐ Deodorant	☐ A guilty pleasure	☐ A brisk walk
☐ Family dinner	☐ An apology	☐ A primal scream	☐ A "Please"
☐ Beds all made	☐ Lottery win	☐ A clean kitchen	☐ A "Thank you"
☐ A pick-me-up	☐ A six-pack	☐ More chocolate	☐ A present
☐ Fireman fantasy	☐ Dust bunny eradication	☐ A foot rub	☐ My prince to come
☐ The toothpaste capped	☐ A parking spot	☐ Chores completed	☐ A big bowl of ice cream
☐ A good hair day	☐ No tears	☐ Snuggle time	☐ A serenade
☐ Less laundry	☐ Stain-free day	☐ A good laugh	☐ Grace under pressure
☐ Window-shopping	☐ A haiku	☐ Clean sheets	☐ Mind over matter
☐ Complete obedience	☐ Cuddling	☐ A glass of bubbly	☐ Good will
☐ A chuckle	☐ Coddling	☐ Better neighbors	☐ Flowers
☐ Clean children	☐ A blowout	☐ To hear I'm cool	☐ A miracle
☐ A sincere compliment	☐ An empty dishwasher	☐ To hear I'm hot	☐ Some "me" time
☐ Mani-pedi	☐ You to put on a sweater	☐ Yoga	☐ A good cry
☐ A shoulder to cry on	☐ A nap	☐ Validation	☐ Girl's night out
☐ A random thoughtful act	☐ More help	☐ Breakfast in bed	☐ Romantic dinner
☐ To feel like a million bucks	☐ Complete silence	☐ Control of remote	☐ Full-time help
☐ To look like a million bucks	☐ Extra cheese	☐ A neck rub	☐ Just a little appreciation
☐ A million bucks	☐ A bra that fits	☐ A big smile	☐ Just you

☐ **PLEASE**   ☐ **PRETTY PLEASE**   ☐ **THANK YOU**   ☐ **OR ELSE**

SIGNATURE (ACTUAL NAME OF MOTHER)   MONTH   DAY   YEAR

"IS IT REALLY SO MUCH TO ASK?"

THINGS MOM REALLY, REALLY, REALLY NEEDS

☐ **SOON**   ☐ **TODAY**   ☐ **RIGHT NOW**   ☐ **FROM NOW ON**

☐ A break	☐ For you to read my mind	☐ Candlelight	☐ Movie night
☐ Less whine	☐ An aspirin	☐ Space	☐ A side of fries
☐ More wine	☐ Some respect	☐ A well-stocked fridge	☐ Some lovin'
☐ Your love	☐ Pizza, toppings my choice	☐ Commiseration	☐ A chauffeur
☐ Chocolate	☐ A good book	☐ To sleep in	☐ Inside voices
☐ A vacation	☐ Work-life balance	☐ A margarita	☐ A little more help
☐ Peace	☐ For you to make dinner	☐ Tantrum absence	☐ Vim
☐ Quiet	☐ A little enthusiasm	☐ The toilet seat down	☐ Vigor
☐ Peace and quiet	☐ To recapture my youth	☐ Someone to take out dog	☐ A good babysitter
☐ A date night	☐ Alone time	☐ Someone to bring in cat	☐ Soft lights
☐ The toilet paper replaced	☐ Alone time in bathroom	☐ A makeover	☐ Soft music
☐ Pampering	☐ Someone to admit I'm right	☐ Costume drama on DVR	☐ Clean clothes
☐ A kiss	☐ A shopping spree	☐ Reality TV on DVR	☐ Time to read
☐ A hug	☐ Attitude of gratitude	☐ Punctuality	☐ A day without dieting
☐ A bear hug	☐ Pie	☐ Endorphin rush	☐ Calm
☐ Someone to listen	☐ A massage	☐ Personal shopper	☐ A friendly phone call
☐ Takeout	☐ An ego massage	☐ Personal schlepper	☐ A day off
☐ A little help	☐ All the answers	☐ A mate to that sock	☐ A smidgen of kindness
☐ To fit into those jeans	☐ Any answer	☐ Time to reflect	☐ A good workout
☐ Privacy	☐ Sweet nothings	☐ A little consideration	☐ A new job
☐ A love note	☐ Personal trainer	☐ Spa day	☐ Even more wine
☐ No complaints	☐ Personal assistant	☐ To be fed grapes	☐ Utter devotion
☐ Hot coffee	☐ A cup of tea	☐ A stiff one	☐ Cupcakes
☐ A hot bath	☐ Therapy	☐ Mother's little helper	☐ Thermostat control
☐ A cold shower	☐ A good night's sleep	☐ A pep talk	☐ A cold drink
☐ Some good gossip	☐ Jewelry	☐ Fewer interruptions	☐ Inner peace
☐ A day in pajamas	☐ To be the center of attention	☐ To win	☐ A day without poop
☐ A day out of sweats	☐ To sit down for a minute	☐ A sugar fix	☐ Sympathy
☐ New shoes	☐ A happy child	☐ Well-behaved inner child	☐ Empathy
☐ A bit of effort	☐ A happy spouse	☐ Well-behaved children	☐ A comfy chair
☐ Barf-free clothing	☐ Praise for my intellect	☐ To get outside	☐ Second helping of dessert
☐ Stress relief	☐ Deodorant	☐ A guilty pleasure	☐ A brisk walk
☐ Family dinner	☐ An apology	☐ A primal scream	☐ A "Please"
☐ Beds all made	☐ Lottery win	☐ A clean kitchen	☐ A "Thank you"
☐ A pick-me-up	☐ A six-pack	☐ More chocolate	☐ A present
☐ Fireman fantasy	☐ Dust bunny eradication	☐ A foot rub	☐ My prince to come
☐ The toothpaste capped	☐ A parking spot	☐ Chores completed	☐ A big bowl of ice cream
☐ A good hair day	☐ No tears	☐ Snuggle time	☐ A serenade
☐ Less laundry	☐ Stain-free day	☐ A good laugh	☐ Grace under pressure
☐ Window-shopping	☐ A haiku	☐ Clean sheets	☐ Mind over matter
☐ Complete obedience	☐ Cuddling	☐ A glass of bubbly	☐ Good will
☐ A chuckle	☐ Coddling	☐ Better neighbors	☐ Flowers
☐ Clean children	☐ A blowout	☐ To hear I'm cool	☐ A miracle
☐ A sincere compliment	☐ An empty dishwasher	☐ To hear I'm hot	☐ Some "me" time
☐ Mani-pedi	☐ You to put on a sweater	☐ Yoga	☐ A good cry
☐ A shoulder to cry on	☐ A nap	☐ Validation	☐ Girl's night out
☐ A random thoughtful act	☐ More help	☐ Breakfast in bed	☐ Romantic dinner
☐ To feel like a million bucks	☐ Complete silence	☐ Control of remote	☐ Full-time help
☐ To look like a million bucks	☐ Extra cheese	☐ A neck rub	☐ Just a little appreciation
☐ A million bucks	☐ A bra that fits	☐ A big smile	☐ Just you

☐ **PLEASE**   ☐ **PRETTY PLEASE**   ☐ **THANK YOU**   ☐ **OR ELSE**

	MONTH	DAY	YEAR
SIGNATURE (ACTUAL NAME OF MOTHER)			

"IS IT REALLY SO MUCH TO ASK?"

THINGS MOM REALLY, REALLY, REALLY NEEDS

☐ **SOON**   ☐ **TODAY**   ☐ **RIGHT NOW**   ☐ **FROM NOW ON**

☐ A break	☐ For you to read my mind	☐ Candlelight	☐ Movie night
☐ Less whine	☐ An aspirin	☐ Space	☐ A side of fries
☐ More wine	☐ Some respect	☐ A well-stocked fridge	☐ Some lovin'
☐ Your love	☐ Pizza, toppings my choice	☐ Commiseration	☐ A chauffeur
☐ Chocolate	☐ A good book	☐ To sleep in	☐ Inside voices
☐ A vacation	☐ Work-life balance	☐ A margarita	☐ A little more help
☐ Peace	☐ For you to make dinner	☐ Tantrum absence	☐ Vim
☐ Quiet	☐ A little enthusiasm	☐ The toilet seat down	☐ Vigor
☐ Peace and quiet	☐ To recapture my youth	☐ Someone to take out dog	☐ A good babysitter
☐ A date night	☐ Alone time	☐ Someone to bring in cat	☐ Soft lights
☐ The toilet paper replaced	☐ Alone time in bathroom	☐ A makeover	☐ Soft music
☐ Pampering	☐ Someone to admit I'm right	☐ Costume drama on DVR	☐ Clean clothes
☐ A kiss	☐ A shopping spree	☐ Reality TV on DVR	☐ Time to read
☐ A hug	☐ Attitude of gratitude	☐ Punctuality	☐ A day without dieting
☐ A bear hug	☐ Pie	☐ Endorphin rush	☐ Calm
☐ Someone to listen	☐ A massage	☐ Personal shopper	☐ A friendly phone call
☐ Takeout	☐ An ego massage	☐ Personal schlepper	☐ A day off
☐ A little help	☐ All the answers	☐ A mate to that sock	☐ A smidgen of kindness
☐ To fit into those jeans	☐ Any answer	☐ Time to reflect	☐ A good workout
☐ Privacy	☐ Sweet nothings	☐ A little consideration	☐ A new job
☐ A love note	☐ Personal trainer	☐ Spa day	☐ Even more wine
☐ No complaints	☐ Personal assistant	☐ To be fed grapes	☐ Utter devotion
☐ Hot coffee	☐ A cup of tea	☐ A stiff one	☐ Cupcakes
☐ A hot bath	☐ Therapy	☐ Mother's little helper	☐ Thermostat control
☐ A cold shower	☐ A good night's sleep	☐ A pep talk	☐ A cold drink
☐ Some good gossip	☐ Jewelry	☐ Fewer interruptions	☐ Inner peace
☐ A day in pajamas	☐ To be the center of attention	☐ To win	☐ A day without poop
☐ A day out of sweats	☐ To sit down for a minute	☐ A sugar fix	☐ Sympathy
☐ New shoes	☐ A happy child	☐ Well-behaved inner child	☐ Empathy
☐ A bit of effort	☐ A happy spouse	☐ Well-behaved children	☐ A comfy chair
☐ Barf-free clothing	☐ Praise for my intellect	☐ To get outside	☐ Second helping of dessert
☐ Stress relief	☐ Deodorant	☐ A guilty pleasure	☐ A brisk walk
☐ Family dinner	☐ An apology	☐ A primal scream	☐ A "Please"
☐ Beds all made	☐ Lottery win	☐ A clean kitchen	☐ A "Thank you"
☐ A pick-me-up	☐ A six-pack	☐ More chocolate	☐ A present
☐ Fireman fantasy	☐ Dust bunny eradication	☐ A foot rub	☐ My prince to come
☐ The toothpaste capped	☐ A parking spot	☐ Chores completed	☐ A big bowl of ice cream
☐ A good hair day	☐ No tears	☐ Snuggle time	☐ A serenade
☐ Less laundry	☐ Stain-free day	☐ A good laugh	☐ Grace under pressure
☐ Window-shopping	☐ A haiku	☐ Clean sheets	☐ Mind over matter
☐ Complete obedience	☐ Cuddling	☐ A glass of bubbly	☐ Good will
☐ A chuckle	☐ Coddling	☐ Better neighbors	☐ Flowers
☐ Clean children	☐ A blowout	☐ To hear I'm cool	☐ A miracle
☐ A sincere compliment	☐ An empty dishwasher	☐ To hear I'm hot	☐ Some "me" time
☐ Mani-pedi	☐ You to put on a sweater	☐ Yoga	☐ A good cry
☐ A shoulder to cry on	☐ A nap	☐ Validation	☐ Girl's night out
☐ A random thoughtful act	☐ More help	☐ Breakfast in bed	☐ Romantic dinner
☐ To feel like a million bucks	☐ Complete silence	☐ Control of remote	☐ Full-time help
☐ To look like a million bucks	☐ Extra cheese	☐ A neck rub	☐ Just a little appreciation
☐ A million bucks	☐ A bra that fits	☐ A big smile	☐ Just you

☐ **PLEASE**   ☐ **PRETTY PLEASE**   ☐ **THANK YOU**   ☐ **OR ELSE**

		MONTH	DAY	YEAR

SIGNATURE (ACTUAL NAME OF MOTHER)

"IS IT REALLY SO MUCH TO ASK?"

THINGS MOM REALLY, REALLY, REALLY NEEDS

☐ SOON ☐ TODAY ☐ RIGHT NOW ☐ FROM NOW ON

SOON	TODAY	RIGHT NOW	FROM NOW ON
☐ A break	☐ For you to read my mind	☐ Candlelight	☐ Movie night
☐ Less whine	☐ An aspirin	☐ Space	☐ A side of fries
☐ More wine	☐ Some respect	☐ A well-stocked fridge	☐ Some lovin'
☐ Your love	☐ Pizza, toppings my choice	☐ Commiseration	☐ A chauffeur
☐ Chocolate	☐ A good book	☐ To sleep in	☐ Inside voices
☐ A vacation	☐ Work-life balance	☐ A margarita	☐ A little more help
☐ Peace	☐ For you to make dinner	☐ Tantrum absence	☐ Vim
☐ Quiet	☐ A little enthusiasm	☐ The toilet seat down	☐ Vigor
☐ Peace and quiet	☐ To recapture my youth	☐ Someone to take out dog	☐ A good babysitter
☐ A date night	☐ Alone time	☐ Someone to bring in cat	☐ Soft lights
☐ The toilet paper replaced	☐ Alone time in bathroom	☐ A makeover	☐ Soft music
☐ Pampering	☐ Someone to admit I'm right	☐ Costume drama on DVR	☐ Clean clothes
☐ A kiss	☐ A shopping spree	☐ Reality TV on DVR	☐ Time to read
☐ A hug	☐ Attitude of gratitude	☐ Punctuality	☐ A day without dieting
☐ A bear hug	☐ Pie	☐ Endorphin rush	☐ Calm
☐ Someone to listen	☐ A massage	☐ Personal shopper	☐ A friendly phone call
☐ Takeout	☐ An ego massage	☐ Personal schlepper	☐ A day off
☐ A little help	☐ All the answers	☐ A mate to that sock	☐ A smidgen of kindness
☐ To fit into those jeans	☐ Any answer	☐ Time to reflect	☐ A good workout
☐ Privacy	☐ Sweet nothings	☐ A little consideration	☐ A new job
☐ A love note	☐ Personal trainer	☐ Spa day	☐ Even more wine
☐ No complaints	☐ Personal assistant	☐ To be fed grapes	☐ Utter devotion
☐ Hot coffee	☐ A cup of tea	☐ A stiff one	☐ Cupcakes
☐ A hot bath	☐ Therapy	☐ Mother's little helper	☐ Thermostat control
☐ A cold shower	☐ A good night's sleep	☐ A pep talk	☐ A cold drink
☐ Some good gossip	☐ Jewelry	☐ Fewer interruptions	☐ Inner peace
☐ A day in pajamas	☐ To be the center of attention	☐ To win	☐ A day without poop
☐ A day out of sweats	☐ To sit down for a minute	☐ A sugar fix	☐ Sympathy
☐ New shoes	☐ A happy child	☐ Well-behaved inner child	☐ Empathy
☐ A bit of effort	☐ A happy spouse	☐ Well-behaved children	☐ A comfy chair
☐ Barf-free clothing	☐ Praise for my intellect	☐ To get outside	☐ Second helping of dessert
☐ Stress relief	☐ Deodorant	☐ A guilty pleasure	☐ A brisk walk
☐ Family dinner	☐ An apology	☐ A primal scream	☐ A "Please"
☐ Beds all made	☐ Lottery win	☐ A clean kitchen	☐ A "Thank you"
☐ A pick-me-up	☐ A six-pack	☐ More chocolate	☐ A present
☐ Fireman fantasy	☐ Dust bunny eradication	☐ A foot rub	☐ My prince to come
☐ The toothpaste capped	☐ A parking spot	☐ Chores completed	☐ A big bowl of ice cream
☐ A good hair day	☐ No tears	☐ Snuggle time	☐ A serenade
☐ Less laundry	☐ Stain-free day	☐ A good laugh	☐ Grace under pressure
☐ Window-shopping	☐ A haiku	☐ Clean sheets	☐ Mind over matter
☐ Complete obedience	☐ Cuddling	☐ A glass of bubbly	☐ Good will
☐ A chuckle	☐ Coddling	☐ Better neighbors	☐ Flowers
☐ Clean children	☐ A blowout	☐ To hear I'm cool	☐ A miracle
☐ A sincere compliment	☐ An empty dishwasher	☐ To hear I'm hot	☐ Some "me" time
☐ Mani-pedi	☐ You to put on a sweater	☐ Yoga	☐ A good cry
☐ A shoulder to cry on	☐ A nap	☐ Validation	☐ Girl's night out
☐ A random thoughtful act	☐ More help	☐ Breakfast in bed	☐ Romantic dinner
☐ To feel like a million bucks	☐ Complete silence	☐ Control of remote	☐ Full-time help
☐ To look like a million bucks	☐ Extra cheese	☐ A neck rub	☐ Just a little appreciation
☐ A million bucks	☐ A bra that fits	☐ A big smile	☐ Just you

☐ PLEASE ☐ PRETTY PLEASE ☐ THANK YOU ☐ OR ELSE

		MONTH	DAY	YEAR
SIGNATURE (ACTUAL NAME OF MOTHER)				

"IS IT REALLY SO MUCH TO ASK?"

THINGS MOM REALLY, REALLY, REALLY NEEDS

☐ **SOON** ☐ **TODAY** ☐ **RIGHT NOW** ☐ **FROM NOW ON**

SOON	TODAY	RIGHT NOW	FROM NOW ON
☐ A break	☐ For you to read my mind	☐ Candlelight	☐ Movie night
☐ Less whine	☐ An aspirin	☐ Space	☐ A side of fries
☐ More wine	☐ Some respect	☐ A well-stocked fridge	☐ Some lovin'
☐ Your love	☐ Pizza, toppings my choice	☐ Commiseration	☐ A chauffeur
☐ Chocolate	☐ A good book	☐ To sleep in	☐ Inside voices
☐ A vacation	☐ Work-life balance	☐ A margarita	☐ A little more help
☐ Peace	☐ For you to make dinner	☐ Tantrum absence	☐ Vim
☐ Quiet	☐ A little enthusiasm	☐ The toilet seat down	☐ Vigor
☐ Peace and quiet	☐ To recapture my youth	☐ Someone to take out dog	☐ A good babysitter
☐ A date night	☐ Alone time	☐ Someone to bring in cat	☐ Soft lights
☐ The toilet paper replaced	☐ Alone time in bathroom	☐ A makeover	☐ Soft music
☐ Pampering	☐ Someone to admit I'm right	☐ Costume drama on DVR	☐ Clean clothes
☐ A kiss	☐ A shopping spree	☐ Reality TV on DVR	☐ Time to read
☐ A hug	☐ Attitude of gratitude	☐ Punctuality	☐ A day without dieting
☐ A bear hug	☐ Pie	☐ Endorphin rush	☐ Calm
☐ Someone to listen	☐ A massage	☐ Personal shopper	☐ A friendly phone call
☐ Takeout	☐ An ego massage	☐ Personal schlepper	☐ A day off
☐ A little help	☐ All the answers	☐ A mate to that sock	☐ A smidgen of kindness
☐ To fit into those jeans	☐ Any answer	☐ Time to reflect	☐ A good workout
☐ Privacy	☐ Sweet nothings	☐ A little consideration	☐ A new job
☐ A love note	☐ Personal trainer	☐ Spa day	☐ Even more wine
☐ No complaints	☐ Personal assistant	☐ To be fed grapes	☐ Utter devotion
☐ Hot coffee	☐ A cup of tea	☐ A stiff one	☐ Cupcakes
☐ A hot bath	☐ Therapy	☐ Mother's little helper	☐ Thermostat control
☐ A cold shower	☐ A good night's sleep	☐ A pep talk	☐ A cold drink
☐ Some good gossip	☐ Jewelry	☐ Fewer interruptions	☐ Inner peace
☐ A day in pajamas	☐ To be the center of attention	☐ To win	☐ A day without poop
☐ A day out of sweats	☐ To sit down for a minute	☐ A sugar fix	☐ Sympathy
☐ New shoes	☐ A happy child	☐ Well-behaved inner child	☐ Empathy
☐ A bit of effort	☐ A happy spouse	☐ Well-behaved children	☐ A comfy chair
☐ Barf-free clothing	☐ Praise for my intellect	☐ To get outside	☐ Second helping of dessert
☐ Stress relief	☐ Deodorant	☐ A guilty pleasure	☐ A brisk walk
☐ Family dinner	☐ An apology	☐ A primal scream	☐ A "Please"
☐ Beds all made	☐ Lottery win	☐ A clean kitchen	☐ A "Thank you"
☐ A pick-me-up	☐ A six-pack	☐ More chocolate	☐ A present
☐ Fireman fantasy	☐ Dust bunny eradication	☐ A foot rub	☐ My prince to come
☐ The toothpaste capped	☐ A parking spot	☐ Chores completed	☐ A big bowl of ice cream
☐ A good hair day	☐ No tears	☐ Snuggle time	☐ A serenade
☐ Less laundry	☐ Stain-free day	☐ A good laugh	☐ Grace under pressure
☐ Window-shopping	☐ A haiku	☐ Clean sheets	☐ Mind over matter
☐ Complete obedience	☐ Cuddling	☐ A glass of bubbly	☐ Good will
☐ A chuckle	☐ Coddling	☐ Better neighbors	☐ Flowers
☐ Clean children	☐ A blowout	☐ To hear I'm cool	☐ A miracle
☐ A sincere compliment	☐ An empty dishwasher	☐ To hear I'm hot	☐ Some "me" time
☐ Mani-pedi	☐ You to put on a sweater	☐ Yoga	☐ A good cry
☐ A shoulder to cry on	☐ A nap	☐ Validation	☐ Girl's night out
☐ A random thoughtful act	☐ More help	☐ Breakfast in bed	☐ Romantic dinner
☐ To feel like a million bucks	☐ Complete silence	☐ Control of remote	☐ Full-time help
☐ To look like a million bucks	☐ Extra cheese	☐ A neck rub	☐ Just a little appreciation
☐ A million bucks	☐ A bra that fits	☐ A big smile	☐ Just you

☐ **PLEASE**   ☐ **PRETTY PLEASE**   ☐ **THANK YOU**   ☐ **OR ELSE**

		MONTH	DAY	YEAR
SIGNATURE (ACTUAL NAME OF MOTHER)				

"IS IT REALLY SO MUCH TO ASK?"

THINGS MOM REALLY, REALLY, REALLY NEEDS

☐ **SOON**   ☐ **TODAY**   ☐ **RIGHT NOW**   ☐ **FROM NOW ON**

SOON	TODAY	RIGHT NOW	FROM NOW ON
☐ A break	☐ For you to read my mind	☐ Candlelight	☐ Movie night
☐ Less whine	☐ An aspirin	☐ Space	☐ A side of fries
☐ More wine	☐ Some respect	☐ A well-stocked fridge	☐ Some lovin'
☐ Your love	☐ Pizza, toppings my choice	☐ Commiseration	☐ A chauffeur
☐ Chocolate	☐ A good book	☐ To sleep in	☐ Inside voices
☐ A vacation	☐ Work-life balance	☐ A margarita	☐ A little more help
☐ Peace	☐ For you to make dinner	☐ Tantrum absence	☐ Vim
☐ Quiet	☐ A little enthusiasm	☐ The toilet seat down	☐ Vigor
☐ Peace and quiet	☐ To recapture my youth	☐ Someone to take out dog	☐ A good babysitter
☐ A date night	☐ Alone time	☐ Someone to bring in cat	☐ Soft lights
☐ The toilet paper replaced	☐ Alone time in bathroom	☐ A makeover	☐ Soft music
☐ Pampering	☐ Someone to admit I'm right	☐ Costume drama on DVR	☐ Clean clothes
☐ A kiss	☐ A shopping spree	☐ Reality TV on DVR	☐ Time to read
☐ A hug	☐ Attitude of gratitude	☐ Punctuality	☐ A day without dieting
☐ A bear hug	☐ Pie	☐ Endorphin rush	☐ Calm
☐ Someone to listen	☐ A massage	☐ Personal shopper	☐ A friendly phone call
☐ Takeout	☐ An ego massage	☐ Personal schlepper	☐ A day off
☐ A little help	☐ All the answers	☐ A mate to that sock	☐ A smidgen of kindness
☐ To fit into those jeans	☐ Any answer	☐ Time to reflect	☐ A good workout
☐ Privacy	☐ Sweet nothings	☐ A little consideration	☐ A new job
☐ A love note	☐ Personal trainer	☐ Spa day	☐ Even more wine
☐ No complaints	☐ Personal assistant	☐ To be fed grapes	☐ Utter devotion
☐ Hot coffee	☐ A cup of tea	☐ A stiff one	☐ Cupcakes
☐ A hot bath	☐ Therapy	☐ Mother's little helper	☐ Thermostat control
☐ A cold shower	☐ A good night's sleep	☐ A pep talk	☐ A cold drink
☐ Some good gossip	☐ Jewelry	☐ Fewer interruptions	☐ Inner peace
☐ A day in pajamas	☐ To be the center of attention	☐ To win	☐ A day without poop
☐ A day out of sweats	☐ To sit down for a minute	☐ A sugar fix	☐ Sympathy
☐ New shoes	☐ A happy child	☐ Well-behaved inner child	☐ Empathy
☐ A bit of effort	☐ A happy spouse	☐ Well-behaved children	☐ A comfy chair
☐ Barf-free clothing	☐ Praise for my intellect	☐ To get outside	☐ Second helping of dessert
☐ Stress relief	☐ Deodorant	☐ A guilty pleasure	☐ A brisk walk
☐ Family dinner	☐ An apology	☐ A primal scream	☐ A "Please"
☐ Beds all made	☐ Lottery win	☐ A clean kitchen	☐ A "Thank you"
☐ A pick-me-up	☐ A six-pack	☐ More chocolate	☐ A present
☐ Fireman fantasy	☐ Dust bunny eradication	☐ A foot rub	☐ My prince to come
☐ The toothpaste capped	☐ A parking spot	☐ Chores completed	☐ A big bowl of ice cream
☐ A good hair day	☐ No tears	☐ Snuggle time	☐ A serenade
☐ Less laundry	☐ Stain-free day	☐ A good laugh	☐ Grace under pressure
☐ Window-shopping	☐ A haiku	☐ Clean sheets	☐ Mind over matter
☐ Complete obedience	☐ Cuddling	☐ A glass of bubbly	☐ Good will
☐ A chuckle	☐ Coddling	☐ Better neighbors	☐ Flowers
☐ Clean children	☐ A blowout	☐ To hear I'm cool	☐ A miracle
☐ A sincere compliment	☐ An empty dishwasher	☐ To hear I'm hot	☐ Some "me" time
☐ Mani-pedi	☐ You to put on a sweater	☐ Yoga	☐ A good cry
☐ A shoulder to cry on	☐ A nap	☐ Validation	☐ Girl's night out
☐ A random thoughtful act	☐ More help	☐ Breakfast in bed	☐ Romantic dinner
☐ To feel like a million bucks	☐ Complete silence	☐ Control of remote	☐ Full-time help
☐ To look like a million bucks	☐ Extra cheese	☐ A neck rub	☐ Just a little appreciation
☐ A million bucks	☐ A bra that fits	☐ A big smile	☐ Just you

☐ **PLEASE**   ☐ **PRETTY PLEASE**   ☐ **THANK YOU**   ☐ **OR ELSE**

				MONTH	DAY	YEAR
SIGNATURE (ACTUAL NAME OF MOTHER)						

"IS IT REALLY SO MUCH TO ASK?"

THINGS MOM REALLY, REALLY, REALLY NEEDS

☐ **SOON**　　☐ **TODAY**　　☐ **RIGHT NOW**　　☐ **FROM NOW ON**

☐ A break	☐ For you to read my mind	☐ Candlelight	☐ Movie night
☐ Less whine	☐ An aspirin	☐ Space	☐ A side of fries
☐ More wine	☐ Some respect	☐ A well-stocked fridge	☐ Some lovin'
☐ Your love	☐ Pizza, toppings my choice	☐ Commiseration	☐ A chauffeur
☐ Chocolate	☐ A good book	☐ To sleep in	☐ Inside voices
☐ A vacation	☐ Work-life balance	☐ A margarita	☐ A little more help
☐ Peace	☐ For you to make dinner	☐ Tantrum absence	☐ Vim
☐ Quiet	☐ A little enthusiasm	☐ The toilet seat down	☐ Vigor
☐ Peace and quiet	☐ To recapture my youth	☐ Someone to take out dog	☐ A good babysitter
☐ A date night	☐ Alone time	☐ Someone to bring in cat	☐ Soft lights
☐ The toilet paper replaced	☐ Alone time in bathroom	☐ A makeover	☐ Soft music
☐ Pampering	☐ Someone to admit I'm right	☐ Costume drama on DVR	☐ Clean clothes
☐ A kiss	☐ A shopping spree	☐ Reality TV on DVR	☐ Time to read
☐ A hug	☐ Attitude of gratitude	☐ Punctuality	☐ A day without dieting
☐ A bear hug	☐ Pie	☐ Endorphin rush	☐ Calm
☐ Someone to listen	☐ A massage	☐ Personal shopper	☐ A friendly phone call
☐ Takeout	☐ An ego massage	☐ Personal schlepper	☐ A day off
☐ A little help	☐ All the answers	☐ A mate to that sock	☐ A smidgen of kindness
☐ To fit into those jeans	☐ Any answer	☐ Time to reflect	☐ A good workout
☐ Privacy	☐ Sweet nothings	☐ A little consideration	☐ A new job
☐ A love note	☐ Personal trainer	☐ Spa day	☐ Even more wine
☐ No complaints	☐ Personal assistant	☐ To be fed grapes	☐ Utter devotion
☐ Hot coffee	☐ A cup of tea	☐ A stiff one	☐ Cupcakes
☐ A hot bath	☐ Therapy	☐ Mother's little helper	☐ Thermostat control
☐ A cold shower	☐ A good night's sleep	☐ A pep talk	☐ A cold drink
☐ Some good gossip	☐ Jewelry	☐ Fewer interruptions	☐ Inner peace
☐ A day in pajamas	☐ To be the center of attention	☐ To win	☐ A day without poop
☐ A day out of sweats	☐ To sit down for a minute	☐ A sugar fix	☐ Sympathy
☐ New shoes	☐ A happy child	☐ Well-behaved inner child	☐ Empathy
☐ A bit of effort	☐ A happy spouse	☐ Well-behaved children	☐ A comfy chair
☐ Barf-free clothing	☐ Praise for my intellect	☐ To get outside	☐ Second helping of dessert
☐ Stress relief	☐ Deodorant	☐ A guilty pleasure	☐ A brisk walk
☐ Family dinner	☐ An apology	☐ A primal scream	☐ A "Please"
☐ Beds all made	☐ Lottery win	☐ A clean kitchen	☐ A "Thank you"
☐ A pick-me-up	☐ A six-pack	☐ More chocolate	☐ A present
☐ Fireman fantasy	☐ Dust bunny eradication	☐ A foot rub	☐ My prince to come
☐ The toothpaste capped	☐ A parking spot	☐ Chores completed	☐ A big bowl of ice cream
☐ A good hair day	☐ No tears	☐ Snuggle time	☐ A serenade
☐ Less laundry	☐ Stain-free day	☐ A good laugh	☐ Grace under pressure
☐ Window-shopping	☐ A haiku	☐ Clean sheets	☐ Mind over matter
☐ Complete obedience	☐ Cuddling	☐ A glass of bubbly	☐ Good will
☐ A chuckle	☐ Coddling	☐ Better neighbors	☐ Flowers
☐ Clean children	☐ A blowout	☐ To hear I'm cool	☐ A miracle
☐ A sincere compliment	☐ An empty dishwasher	☐ To hear I'm hot	☐ Some "me" time
☐ Mani-pedi	☐ You to put on a sweater	☐ Yoga	☐ A good cry
☐ A shoulder to cry on	☐ A nap	☐ Validation	☐ Girl's night out
☐ A random thoughtful act	☐ More help	☐ Breakfast in bed	☐ Romantic dinner
☐ To feel like a million bucks	☐ Complete silence	☐ Control of remote	☐ Full-time help
☐ To look like a million bucks	☐ Extra cheese	☐ A neck rub	☐ Just a little appreciation
☐ A million bucks	☐ A bra that fits	☐ A big smile	☐ Just you

☐ **PLEASE**　　☐ **PRETTY PLEASE**　　☐ **THANK YOU**　　☐ **OR ELSE**

| SIGNATURE (ACTUAL NAME OF MOTHER) | MONTH | DAY | YEAR |

"IS IT REALLY SO MUCH TO ASK?"

THINGS MOM REALLY, REALLY, REALLY NEEDS

☐ **SOON**   ☐ **TODAY**   ☐ **RIGHT NOW**   ☐ **FROM NOW ON**

SOON	TODAY	RIGHT NOW	FROM NOW ON
☐ A break	☐ For you to read my mind	☐ Candlelight	☐ Movie night
☐ Less whine	☐ An aspirin	☐ Space	☐ A side of fries
☐ More wine	☐ Some respect	☐ A well-stocked fridge	☐ Some lovin'
☐ Your love	☐ Pizza, toppings my choice	☐ Commiseration	☐ A chauffeur
☐ Chocolate	☐ A good book	☐ To sleep in	☐ Inside voices
☐ A vacation	☐ Work-life balance	☐ A margarita	☐ A little more help
☐ Peace	☐ For you to make dinner	☐ Tantrum absence	☐ Vim
☐ Quiet	☐ A little enthusiasm	☐ The toilet seat down	☐ Vigor
☐ Peace and quiet	☐ To recapture my youth	☐ Someone to take out dog	☐ A good babysitter
☐ A date night	☐ Alone time	☐ Someone to bring in cat	☐ Soft lights
☐ The toilet paper replaced	☐ Alone time in bathroom	☐ A makeover	☐ Soft music
☐ Pampering	☐ Someone to admit I'm right	☐ Costume drama on DVR	☐ Clean clothes
☐ A kiss	☐ A shopping spree	☐ Reality TV on DVR	☐ Time to read
☐ A hug	☐ Attitude of gratitude	☐ Punctuality	☐ A day without dieting
☐ A bear hug	☐ Pie	☐ Endorphin rush	☐ Calm
☐ Someone to listen	☐ A massage	☐ Personal shopper	☐ A friendly phone call
☐ Takeout	☐ An ego massage	☐ Personal schlepper	☐ A day off
☐ A little help	☐ All the answers	☐ A mate to that sock	☐ A smidgen of kindness
☐ To fit into those jeans	☐ Any answer	☐ Time to reflect	☐ A good workout
☐ Privacy	☐ Sweet nothings	☐ A little consideration	☐ A new job
☐ A love note	☐ Personal trainer	☐ Spa day	☐ Even more wine
☐ No complaints	☐ Personal assistant	☐ To be fed grapes	☐ Utter devotion
☐ Hot coffee	☐ A cup of tea	☐ A stiff one	☐ Cupcakes
☐ A hot bath	☐ Therapy	☐ Mother's little helper	☐ Thermostat control
☐ A cold shower	☐ A good night's sleep	☐ A pep talk	☐ A cold drink
☐ Some good gossip	☐ Jewelry	☐ Fewer interruptions	☐ Inner peace
☐ A day in pajamas	☐ To be the center of attention	☐ To win	☐ A day without poop
☐ A day out of sweats	☐ To sit down for a minute	☐ A sugar fix	☐ Sympathy
☐ New shoes	☐ A happy child	☐ Well-behaved inner child	☐ Empathy
☐ A bit of effort	☐ A happy spouse	☐ Well-behaved children	☐ A comfy chair
☐ Barf-free clothing	☐ Praise for my intellect	☐ To get outside	☐ Second helping of dessert
☐ Stress relief	☐ Deodorant	☐ A guilty pleasure	☐ A brisk walk
☐ Family dinner	☐ An apology	☐ A primal scream	☐ A "Please"
☐ Beds all made	☐ Lottery win	☐ A clean kitchen	☐ A "Thank you"
☐ A pick-me-up	☐ A six-pack	☐ More chocolate	☐ A present
☐ Fireman fantasy	☐ Dust bunny eradication	☐ A foot rub	☐ My prince to come
☐ The toothpaste capped	☐ A parking spot	☐ Chores completed	☐ A big bowl of ice cream
☐ A good hair day	☐ No tears	☐ Snuggle time	☐ A serenade
☐ Less laundry	☐ Stain-free day	☐ A good laugh	☐ Grace under pressure
☐ Window-shopping	☐ A haiku	☐ Clean sheets	☐ Mind over matter
☐ Complete obedience	☐ Cuddling	☐ A glass of bubbly	☐ Good will
☐ A chuckle	☐ Coddling	☐ Better neighbors	☐ Flowers
☐ Clean children	☐ A blowout	☐ To hear I'm cool	☐ A miracle
☐ A sincere compliment	☐ An empty dishwasher	☐ To hear I'm hot	☐ Some "me" time
☐ Mani-pedi	☐ You to put on a sweater	☐ Yoga	☐ A good cry
☐ A shoulder to cry on	☐ A nap	☐ Validation	☐ Girl's night out
☐ A random thoughtful act	☐ More help	☐ Breakfast in bed	☐ Romantic dinner
☐ To feel like a million bucks	☐ Complete silence	☐ Control of remote	☐ Full-time help
☐ To look like a million bucks	☐ Extra cheese	☐ A neck rub	☐ Just a little appreciation
☐ A million bucks	☐ A bra that fits	☐ A big smile	☐ Just you

☐ **PLEASE**   ☐ **PRETTY PLEASE**   ☐ **THANK YOU**   ☐ **OR ELSE**

SIGNATURE (ACTUAL NAME OF MOTHER) | MONTH | DAY | YEAR |

"IS IT REALLY SO MUCH TO ASK?"

THINGS MOM REALLY, REALLY, REALLY NEEDS

☐ **SOON**　　☐ **TODAY**　　☐ **RIGHT NOW**　　☐ **FROM NOW ON**

SOON	TODAY	RIGHT NOW	FROM NOW ON
☐ A break	☐ For you to read my mind	☐ Candlelight	☐ Movie night
☐ Less whine	☐ An aspirin	☐ Space	☐ A side of fries
☐ More wine	☐ Some respect	☐ A well-stocked fridge	☐ Some lovin'
☐ Your love	☐ Pizza, toppings my choice	☐ Commiseration	☐ A chauffeur
☐ Chocolate	☐ A good book	☐ To sleep in	☐ Inside voices
☐ A vacation	☐ Work-life balance	☐ A margarita	☐ A little more help
☐ Peace	☐ For you to make dinner	☐ Tantrum absence	☐ Vim
☐ Quiet	☐ A little enthusiasm	☐ The toilet seat down	☐ Vigor
☐ Peace and quiet	☐ To recapture my youth	☐ Someone to take out dog	☐ A good babysitter
☐ A date night	☐ Alone time	☐ Someone to bring in cat	☐ Soft lights
☐ The toilet paper replaced	☐ Alone time in bathroom	☐ A makeover	☐ Soft music
☐ Pampering	☐ Someone to admit I'm right	☐ Costume drama on DVR	☐ Clean clothes
☐ A kiss	☐ A shopping spree	☐ Reality TV on DVR	☐ Time to read
☐ A hug	☐ Attitude of gratitude	☐ Punctuality	☐ A day without dieting
☐ A bear hug	☐ Pie	☐ Endorphin rush	☐ Calm
☐ Someone to listen	☐ A massage	☐ Personal shopper	☐ A friendly phone call
☐ Takeout	☐ An ego massage	☐ Personal schlepper	☐ A day off
☐ A little help	☐ All the answers	☐ A mate to that sock	☐ A smidgen of kindness
☐ To fit into those jeans	☐ Any answer	☐ Time to reflect	☐ A good workout
☐ Privacy	☐ Sweet nothings	☐ A little consideration	☐ A new job
☐ A love note	☐ Personal trainer	☐ Spa day	☐ Even more wine
☐ No complaints	☐ Personal assistant	☐ To be fed grapes	☐ Utter devotion
☐ Hot coffee	☐ A cup of tea	☐ A stiff one	☐ Cupcakes
☐ A hot bath	☐ Therapy	☐ Mother's little helper	☐ Thermostat control
☐ A cold shower	☐ A good night's sleep	☐ A pep talk	☐ A cold drink
☐ Some good gossip	☐ Jewelry	☐ Fewer interruptions	☐ Inner peace
☐ A day in pajamas	☐ To be the center of attention	☐ To win	☐ A day without poop
☐ A day out of sweats	☐ To sit down for a minute	☐ A sugar fix	☐ Sympathy
☐ New shoes	☐ A happy child	☐ Well-behaved inner child	☐ Empathy
☐ A bit of effort	☐ A happy spouse	☐ Well-behaved children	☐ A comfy chair
☐ Barf-free clothing	☐ Praise for my intellect	☐ To get outside	☐ Second helping of dessert
☐ Stress relief	☐ Deodorant	☐ A guilty pleasure	☐ A brisk walk
☐ Family dinner	☐ An apology	☐ A primal scream	☐ A "Please"
☐ Beds all made	☐ Lottery win	☐ A clean kitchen	☐ A "Thank you"
☐ A pick-me-up	☐ A six-pack	☐ More chocolate	☐ A present
☐ Fireman fantasy	☐ Dust bunny eradication	☐ A foot rub	☐ My prince to come
☐ The toothpaste capped	☐ A parking spot	☐ Chores completed	☐ A big bowl of ice cream
☐ A good hair day	☐ No tears	☐ Snuggle time	☐ A serenade
☐ Less laundry	☐ Stain-free day	☐ A good laugh	☐ Grace under pressure
☐ Window-shopping	☐ A haiku	☐ Clean sheets	☐ Mind over matter
☐ Complete obedience	☐ Cuddling	☐ A glass of bubbly	☐ Good will
☐ A chuckle	☐ Coddling	☐ Better neighbors	☐ Flowers
☐ Clean children	☐ A blowout	☐ To hear I'm cool	☐ A miracle
☐ A sincere compliment	☐ An empty dishwasher	☐ To hear I'm hot	☐ Some "me" time
☐ Mani-pedi	☐ You to put on a sweater	☐ Yoga	☐ A good cry
☐ A shoulder to cry on	☐ A nap	☐ Validation	☐ Girl's night out
☐ A random thoughtful act	☐ More help	☐ Breakfast in bed	☐ Romantic dinner
☐ To feel like a million bucks	☐ Complete silence	☐ Control of remote	☐ Full-time help
☐ To look like a million bucks	☐ Extra cheese	☐ A neck rub	☐ Just a little appreciation
☐ A million bucks	☐ A bra that fits	☐ A big smile	☐ Just you

☐ **PLEASE**　　☐ **PRETTY PLEASE**　　☐ **THANK YOU**　　☐ **OR ELSE**

SIGNATURE (ACTUAL NAME OF MOTHER)　　MONTH　DAY　YEAR

"IS IT REALLY SO MUCH TO ASK?"

THINGS MOM REALLY, REALLY, REALLY NEEDS

☐ **SOON**   ☐ **TODAY**   ☐ **RIGHT NOW**   ☐ **FROM NOW ON**

SOON	TODAY	RIGHT NOW	FROM NOW ON
☐ A break	☐ For you to read my mind	☐ Candlelight	☐ Movie night
☐ Less whine	☐ An aspirin	☐ Space	☐ A side of fries
☐ More wine	☐ Some respect	☐ A well-stocked fridge	☐ Some lovin'
☐ Your love	☐ Pizza, toppings my choice	☐ Commiseration	☐ A chauffeur
☐ Chocolate	☐ A good book	☐ To sleep in	☐ Inside voices
☐ A vacation	☐ Work-life balance	☐ A margarita	☐ A little more help
☐ Peace	☐ For you to make dinner	☐ Tantrum absence	☐ Vim
☐ Quiet	☐ A little enthusiasm	☐ The toilet seat down	☐ Vigor
☐ Peace and quiet	☐ To recapture my youth	☐ Someone to take out dog	☐ A good babysitter
☐ A date night	☐ Alone time	☐ Someone to bring in cat	☐ Soft lights
☐ The toilet paper replaced	☐ Alone time in bathroom	☐ A makeover	☐ Soft music
☐ Pampering	☐ Someone to admit I'm right	☐ Costume drama on DVR	☐ Clean clothes
☐ A kiss	☐ A shopping spree	☐ Reality TV on DVR	☐ Time to read
☐ A hug	☐ Attitude of gratitude	☐ Punctuality	☐ A day without dieting
☐ A bear hug	☐ Pie	☐ Endorphin rush	☐ Calm
☐ Someone to listen	☐ A massage	☐ Personal shopper	☐ A friendly phone call
☐ Takeout	☐ An ego massage	☐ Personal schlepper	☐ A day off
☐ A little help	☐ All the answers	☐ A mate to that sock	☐ A smidgen of kindness
☐ To fit into those jeans	☐ Any answer	☐ Time to reflect	☐ A good workout
☐ Privacy	☐ Sweet nothings	☐ A little consideration	☐ A new job
☐ A love note	☐ Personal trainer	☐ Spa day	☐ Even more wine
☐ No complaints	☐ Personal assistant	☐ To be fed grapes	☐ Utter devotion
☐ Hot coffee	☐ A cup of tea	☐ A stiff one	☐ Cupcakes
☐ A hot bath	☐ Therapy	☐ Mother's little helper	☐ Thermostat control
☐ A cold shower	☐ A good night's sleep	☐ A pep talk	☐ A cold drink
☐ Some good gossip	☐ Jewelry	☐ Fewer interruptions	☐ Inner peace
☐ A day in pajamas	☐ To be the center of attention	☐ To win	☐ A day without poop
☐ A day out of sweats	☐ To sit down for a minute	☐ A sugar fix	☐ Sympathy
☐ New shoes	☐ A happy child	☐ Well-behaved inner child	☐ Empathy
☐ A bit of effort	☐ A happy spouse	☐ Well-behaved children	☐ A comfy chair
☐ Barf-free clothing	☐ Praise for my intellect	☐ To get outside	☐ Second helping of dessert
☐ Stress relief	☐ Deodorant	☐ A guilty pleasure	☐ A brisk walk
☐ Family dinner	☐ An apology	☐ A primal scream	☐ A "Please"
☐ Beds all made	☐ Lottery win	☐ A clean kitchen	☐ A "Thank you"
☐ A pick-me-up	☐ A six-pack	☐ More chocolate	☐ A present
☐ Fireman fantasy	☐ Dust bunny eradication	☐ A foot rub	☐ My prince to come
☐ The toothpaste capped	☐ A parking spot	☐ Chores completed	☐ A big bowl of ice cream
☐ A good hair day	☐ No tears	☐ Snuggle time	☐ A serenade
☐ Less laundry	☐ Stain-free day	☐ A good laugh	☐ Grace under pressure
☐ Window-shopping	☐ A haiku	☐ Clean sheets	☐ Mind over matter
☐ Complete obedience	☐ Cuddling	☐ A glass of bubbly	☐ Good will
☐ A chuckle	☐ Coddling	☐ Better neighbors	☐ Flowers
☐ Clean children	☐ A blowout	☐ To hear I'm cool	☐ A miracle
☐ A sincere compliment	☐ An empty dishwasher	☐ To hear I'm hot	☐ Some "me" time
☐ Mani-pedi	☐ You to put on a sweater	☐ Yoga	☐ A good cry
☐ A shoulder to cry on	☐ A nap	☐ Validation	☐ Girl's night out
☐ A random thoughtful act	☐ More help	☐ Breakfast in bed	☐ Romantic dinner
☐ To feel like a million bucks	☐ Complete silence	☐ Control of remote	☐ Full-time help
☐ To look like a million bucks	☐ Extra cheese	☐ A neck rub	☐ Just a little appreciation
☐ A million bucks	☐ A bra that fits	☐ A big smile	☐ Just you

☐ **PLEASE**   ☐ **PRETTY PLEASE**   ☐ **THANK YOU**   ☐ **OR ELSE**

SIGNATURE (ACTUAL NAME OF MOTHER) | MONTH | DAY | YEAR

"IS IT REALLY SO MUCH TO ASK?"

THINGS MOM REALLY, REALLY, REALLY NEEDS

☐ **SOON** ☐ **TODAY** ☐ **RIGHT NOW** ☐ **FROM NOW ON**

SOON	TODAY	RIGHT NOW	FROM NOW ON
☐ A break	☐ For you to read my mind	☐ Candlelight	☐ Movie night
☐ Less whine	☐ An aspirin	☐ Space	☐ A side of fries
☐ More wine	☐ Some respect	☐ A well-stocked fridge	☐ Some lovin'
☐ Your love	☐ Pizza, toppings my choice	☐ Commiseration	☐ A chauffeur
☐ Chocolate	☐ A good book	☐ To sleep in	☐ Inside voices
☐ A vacation	☐ Work-life balance	☐ A margarita	☐ A little more help
☐ Peace	☐ For you to make dinner	☐ Tantrum absence	☐ Vim
☐ Quiet	☐ A little enthusiasm	☐ The toilet seat down	☐ Vigor
☐ Peace and quiet	☐ To recapture my youth	☐ Someone to take out dog	☐ A good babysitter
☐ A date night	☐ Alone time	☐ Someone to bring in cat	☐ Soft lights
☐ The toilet paper replaced	☐ Alone time in bathroom	☐ A makeover	☐ Soft music
☐ Pampering	☐ Someone to admit I'm right	☐ Costume drama on DVR	☐ Clean clothes
☐ A kiss	☐ A shopping spree	☐ Reality TV on DVR	☐ Time to read
☐ A hug	☐ Attitude of gratitude	☐ Punctuality	☐ A day without dieting
☐ A bear hug	☐ Pie	☐ Endorphin rush	☐ Calm
☐ Someone to listen	☐ A massage	☐ Personal shopper	☐ A friendly phone call
☐ Takeout	☐ An ego massage	☐ Personal schlepper	☐ A day off
☐ A little help	☐ All the answers	☐ A mate to that sock	☐ A smidgen of kindness
☐ To fit into those jeans	☐ Any answer	☐ Time to reflect	☐ A good workout
☐ Privacy	☐ Sweet nothings	☐ A little consideration	☐ A new job
☐ A love note	☐ Personal trainer	☐ Spa day	☐ Even more wine
☐ No complaints	☐ Personal assistant	☐ To be fed grapes	☐ Utter devotion
☐ Hot coffee	☐ A cup of tea	☐ A stiff one	☐ Cupcakes
☐ A hot bath	☐ Therapy	☐ Mother's little helper	☐ Thermostat control
☐ A cold shower	☐ A good night's sleep	☐ A pep talk	☐ A cold drink
☐ Some good gossip	☐ Jewelry	☐ Fewer interruptions	☐ Inner peace
☐ A day in pajamas	☐ To be the center of attention	☐ To win	☐ A day without poop
☐ A day out of sweats	☐ To sit down for a minute	☐ A sugar fix	☐ Sympathy
☐ New shoes	☐ A happy child	☐ Well-behaved inner child	☐ Empathy
☐ A bit of effort	☐ A happy spouse	☐ Well-behaved children	☐ A comfy chair
☐ Barf-free clothing	☐ Praise for my intellect	☐ To get outside	☐ Second helping of dessert
☐ Stress relief	☐ Deodorant	☐ A guilty pleasure	☐ A brisk walk
☐ Family dinner	☐ An apology	☐ A primal scream	☐ A "Please"
☐ Beds all made	☐ Lottery win	☐ A clean kitchen	☐ A "Thank you"
☐ A pick-me-up	☐ A six-pack	☐ More chocolate	☐ A present
☐ Fireman fantasy	☐ Dust bunny eradication	☐ A foot rub	☐ My prince to come
☐ The toothpaste capped	☐ A parking spot	☐ Chores completed	☐ A big bowl of ice cream
☐ A good hair day	☐ No tears	☐ Snuggle time	☐ A serenade
☐ Less laundry	☐ Stain-free day	☐ A good laugh	☐ Grace under pressure
☐ Window-shopping	☐ A haiku	☐ Clean sheets	☐ Mind over matter
☐ Complete obedience	☐ Cuddling	☐ A glass of bubbly	☐ Good will
☐ A chuckle	☐ Coddling	☐ Better neighbors	☐ Flowers
☐ Clean children	☐ A blowout	☐ To hear I'm cool	☐ A miracle
☐ A sincere compliment	☐ An empty dishwasher	☐ To hear I'm hot	☐ Some "me" time
☐ Mani-pedi	☐ You to put on a sweater	☐ Yoga	☐ A good cry
☐ A shoulder to cry on	☐ A nap	☐ Validation	☐ Girl's night out
☐ A random thoughtful act	☐ More help	☐ Breakfast in bed	☐ Romantic dinner
☐ To feel like a million bucks	☐ Complete silence	☐ Control of remote	☐ Full-time help
☐ To look like a million bucks	☐ Extra cheese	☐ A neck rub	☐ Just a little appreciation
☐ A million bucks	☐ A bra that fits	☐ A big smile	☐ Just you

☐ **PLEASE** ☐ **PRETTY PLEASE** ☐ **THANK YOU** ☐ **OR ELSE**

		MONTH	DAY	YEAR
SIGNATURE (ACTUAL NAME OF MOTHER)				

"IS IT REALLY SO MUCH TO ASK?"

KNOCKKNOCKSTUFF.COM ■ © 2014 WHO'S THERE INC.

THINGS MOM REALLY, REALLY, REALLY NEEDS

☐ **SOON**   ☐ **TODAY**   ☐ **RIGHT NOW**   ☐ **FROM NOW ON**

SOON	TODAY	RIGHT NOW	FROM NOW ON
☐ A break	☐ For you to read my mind	☐ Candlelight	☐ Movie night
☐ Less whine	☐ An aspirin	☐ Space	☐ A side of fries
☐ More wine	☐ Some respect	☐ A well-stocked fridge	☐ Some lovin'
☐ Your love	☐ Pizza, toppings my choice	☐ Commiseration	☐ A chauffeur
☐ Chocolate	☐ A good book	☐ To sleep in	☐ Inside voices
☐ A vacation	☐ Work-life balance	☐ A margarita	☐ A little more help
☐ Peace	☐ For you to make dinner	☐ Tantrum absence	☐ Vim
☐ Quiet	☐ A little enthusiasm	☐ The toilet seat down	☐ Vigor
☐ Peace and quiet	☐ To recapture my youth	☐ Someone to take out dog	☐ A good babysitter
☐ A date night	☐ Alone time	☐ Someone to bring in cat	☐ Soft lights
☐ The toilet paper replaced	☐ Alone time in bathroom	☐ A makeover	☐ Soft music
☐ Pampering	☐ Someone to admit I'm right	☐ Costume drama on DVR	☐ Clean clothes
☐ A kiss	☐ A shopping spree	☐ Reality TV on DVR	☐ Time to read
☐ A hug	☐ Attitude of gratitude	☐ Punctuality	☐ A day without dieting
☐ A bear hug	☐ Pie	☐ Endorphin rush	☐ Calm
☐ Someone to listen	☐ A massage	☐ Personal shopper	☐ A friendly phone call
☐ Takeout	☐ An ego massage	☐ Personal schlepper	☐ A day off
☐ A little help	☐ All the answers	☐ A mate to that sock	☐ A smidgen of kindness
☐ To fit into those jeans	☐ Any answer	☐ Time to reflect	☐ A good workout
☐ Privacy	☐ Sweet nothings	☐ A little consideration	☐ A new job
☐ A love note	☐ Personal trainer	☐ Spa day	☐ Even more wine
☐ No complaints	☐ Personal assistant	☐ To be fed grapes	☐ Utter devotion
☐ Hot coffee	☐ A cup of tea	☐ A stiff one	☐ Cupcakes
☐ A hot bath	☐ Therapy	☐ Mother's little helper	☐ Thermostat control
☐ A cold shower	☐ A good night's sleep	☐ A pep talk	☐ A cold drink
☐ Some good gossip	☐ Jewelry	☐ Fewer interruptions	☐ Inner peace
☐ A day in pajamas	☐ To be the center of attention	☐ To win	☐ A day without poop
☐ A day out of sweats	☐ To sit down for a minute	☐ A sugar fix	☐ Sympathy
☐ New shoes	☐ A happy child	☐ Well-behaved inner child	☐ Empathy
☐ A bit of effort	☐ A happy spouse	☐ Well-behaved children	☐ A comfy chair
☐ Barf-free clothing	☐ Praise for my intellect	☐ To get outside	☐ Second helping of dessert
☐ Stress relief	☐ Deodorant	☐ A guilty pleasure	☐ A brisk walk
☐ Family dinner	☐ An apology	☐ A primal scream	☐ A "Please"
☐ Beds all made	☐ Lottery win	☐ A clean kitchen	☐ A "Thank you"
☐ A pick-me-up	☐ A six-pack	☐ More chocolate	☐ A present
☐ Fireman fantasy	☐ Dust bunny eradication	☐ A foot rub	☐ My prince to come
☐ The toothpaste capped	☐ A parking spot	☐ Chores completed	☐ A big bowl of ice cream
☐ A good hair day	☐ No tears	☐ Snuggle time	☐ A serenade
☐ Less laundry	☐ Stain-free day	☐ A good laugh	☐ Grace under pressure
☐ Window-shopping	☐ A haiku	☐ Clean sheets	☐ Mind over matter
☐ Complete obedience	☐ Cuddling	☐ A glass of bubbly	☐ Good will
☐ A chuckle	☐ Coddling	☐ Better neighbors	☐ Flowers
☐ Clean children	☐ A blowout	☐ To hear I'm cool	☐ A miracle
☐ A sincere compliment	☐ An empty dishwasher	☐ To hear I'm hot	☐ Some "me" time
☐ Mani-pedi	☐ You to put on a sweater	☐ Yoga	☐ A good cry
☐ A shoulder to cry on	☐ A nap	☐ Validation	☐ Girl's night out
☐ A random thoughtful act	☐ More help	☐ Breakfast in bed	☐ Romantic dinner
☐ To feel like a million bucks	☐ Complete silence	☐ Control of remote	☐ Full-time help
☐ To look like a million bucks	☐ Extra cheese	☐ A neck rub	☐ Just a little appreciation
☐ A million bucks	☐ A bra that fits	☐ A big smile	☐ Just you

☐ **PLEASE**   ☐ **PRETTY PLEASE**   ☐ **THANK YOU**   ☐ **OR ELSE**

SIGNATURE (ACTUAL NAME OF MOTHER)	MONTH	DAY	YEAR

"IS IT REALLY SO MUCH TO ASK?"

KNOCKKNOCKSTUFF.COM • © 2014 WHO'S THERE INC.

THINGS MOM REALLY, REALLY, REALLY NEEDS

☐ **SOON** ☐ **TODAY** ☐ **RIGHT NOW** ☐ **FROM NOW ON**

☐ A break	☐ For you to read my mind	☐ Candlelight	☐ Movie night
☐ Less whine	☐ An aspirin	☐ Space	☐ A side of fries
☐ More wine	☐ Some respect	☐ A well-stocked fridge	☐ Some lovin'
☐ Your love	☐ Pizza, toppings my choice	☐ Commiseration	☐ A chauffeur
☐ Chocolate	☐ A good book	☐ To sleep in	☐ Inside voices
☐ A vacation	☐ Work-life balance	☐ A margarita	☐ A little more help
☐ Peace	☐ For you to make dinner	☐ Tantrum absence	☐ Vim
☐ Quiet	☐ A little enthusiasm	☐ The toilet seat down	☐ Vigor
☐ Peace and quiet	☐ To recapture my youth	☐ Someone to take out dog	☐ A good babysitter
☐ A date night	☐ Alone time	☐ Someone to bring in cat	☐ Soft lights
☐ The toilet paper replaced	☐ Alone time in bathroom	☐ A makeover	☐ Soft music
☐ Pampering	☐ Someone to admit I'm right	☐ Costume drama on DVR	☐ Clean clothes
☐ A kiss	☐ A shopping spree	☐ Reality TV on DVR	☐ Time to read
☐ A hug	☐ Attitude of gratitude	☐ Punctuality	☐ A day without dieting
☐ A bear hug	☐ Pie	☐ Endorphin rush	☐ Calm
☐ Someone to listen	☐ A massage	☐ Personal shopper	☐ A friendly phone call
☐ Takeout	☐ An ego massage	☐ Personal schlepper	☐ A day off
☐ A little help	☐ All the answers	☐ A mate to that sock	☐ A smidgen of kindness
☐ To fit into those jeans	☐ Any answer	☐ Time to reflect	☐ A good workout
☐ Privacy	☐ Sweet nothings	☐ A little consideration	☐ A new job
☐ A love note	☐ Personal trainer	☐ Spa day	☐ Even more wine
☐ No complaints	☐ Personal assistant	☐ To be fed grapes	☐ Utter devotion
☐ Hot coffee	☐ A cup of tea	☐ A stiff one	☐ Cupcakes
☐ A hot bath	☐ Therapy	☐ Mother's little helper	☐ Thermostat control
☐ A cold shower	☐ A good night's sleep	☐ A pep talk	☐ A cold drink
☐ Some good gossip	☐ Jewelry	☐ Fewer interruptions	☐ Inner peace
☐ A day in pajamas	☐ To be the center of attention	☐ To win	☐ A day without poop
☐ A day out of sweats	☐ To sit down for a minute	☐ A sugar fix	☐ Sympathy
☐ New shoes	☐ A happy child	☐ Well-behaved inner child	☐ Empathy
☐ A bit of effort	☐ A happy spouse	☐ Well-behaved children	☐ A comfy chair
☐ Barf-free clothing	☐ Praise for my intellect	☐ To get outside	☐ Second helping of dessert
☐ Stress relief	☐ Deodorant	☐ A guilty pleasure	☐ A brisk walk
☐ Family dinner	☐ An apology	☐ A primal scream	☐ A "Please"
☐ Beds all made	☐ Lottery win	☐ A clean kitchen	☐ A "Thank you"
☐ A pick-me-up	☐ A six-pack	☐ More chocolate	☐ A present
☐ Fireman fantasy	☐ Dust bunny eradication	☐ A foot rub	☐ My prince to come
☐ The toothpaste capped	☐ A parking spot	☐ Chores completed	☐ A big bowl of ice cream
☐ A good hair day	☐ No tears	☐ Snuggle time	☐ A serenade
☐ Less laundry	☐ Stain-free day	☐ A good laugh	☐ Grace under pressure
☐ Window-shopping	☐ A haiku	☐ Clean sheets	☐ Mind over matter
☐ Complete obedience	☐ Cuddling	☐ A glass of bubbly	☐ Good will
☐ A chuckle	☐ Coddling	☐ Better neighbors	☐ Flowers
☐ Clean children	☐ A blowout	☐ To hear I'm cool	☐ A miracle
☐ A sincere compliment	☐ An empty dishwasher	☐ To hear I'm hot	☐ Some "me" time
☐ Mani-pedi	☐ You to put on a sweater	☐ Yoga	☐ A good cry
☐ A shoulder to cry on	☐ A nap	☐ Validation	☐ Girl's night out
☐ A random thoughtful act	☐ More help	☐ Breakfast in bed	☐ Romantic dinner
☐ To feel like a million bucks	☐ Complete silence	☐ Control of remote	☐ Full-time help
☐ To look like a million bucks	☐ Extra cheese	☐ A neck rub	☐ Just a little appreciation
☐ A million bucks	☐ A bra that fits	☐ A big smile	☐ Just you

☐ **PLEASE** ☐ **PRETTY PLEASE** ☐ **THANK YOU** ☐ **OR ELSE**

SIGNATURE (ACTUAL NAME OF MOTHER)

MONTH	DAY	YEAR

"IS IT REALLY SO MUCH TO ASK?"

KNOCKKNOCKSTUFF.COM • © 2014 WHO'S THERE INC.

THINGS MOM REALLY, REALLY, REALLY NEEDS

☐ **SOON**   ☐ **TODAY**   ☐ **RIGHT NOW**   ☐ **FROM NOW ON**

SOON	TODAY	RIGHT NOW	FROM NOW ON
☐ A break	☐ For you to read my mind	☐ Candlelight	☐ Movie night
☐ Less whine	☐ An aspirin	☐ Space	☐ A side of fries
☐ More wine	☐ Some respect	☐ A well-stocked fridge	☐ Some lovin'
☐ Your love	☐ Pizza, toppings my choice	☐ Commiseration	☐ A chauffeur
☐ Chocolate	☐ A good book	☐ To sleep in	☐ Inside voices
☐ A vacation	☐ Work-life balance	☐ A margarita	☐ A little more help
☐ Peace	☐ For you to make dinner	☐ Tantrum absence	☐ Vim
☐ Quiet	☐ A little enthusiasm	☐ The toilet seat down	☐ Vigor
☐ Peace and quiet	☐ To recapture my youth	☐ Someone to take out dog	☐ A good babysitter
☐ A date night	☐ Alone time	☐ Someone to bring in cat	☐ Soft lights
☐ The toilet paper replaced	☐ Alone time in bathroom	☐ A makeover	☐ Soft music
☐ Pampering	☐ Someone to admit I'm right	☐ Costume drama on DVR	☐ Clean clothes
☐ A kiss	☐ A shopping spree	☐ Reality TV on DVR	☐ Time to read
☐ A hug	☐ Attitude of gratitude	☐ Punctuality	☐ A day without dieting
☐ A bear hug	☐ Pie	☐ Endorphin rush	☐ Calm
☐ Someone to listen	☐ A massage	☐ Personal shopper	☐ A friendly phone call
☐ Takeout	☐ An ego massage	☐ Personal schlepper	☐ A day off
☐ A little help	☐ All the answers	☐ A mate to that sock	☐ A smidgen of kindness
☐ To fit into those jeans	☐ Any answer	☐ Time to reflect	☐ A good workout
☐ Privacy	☐ Sweet nothings	☐ A little consideration	☐ A new job
☐ A love note	☐ Personal trainer	☐ Spa day	☐ Even more wine
☐ No complaints	☐ Personal assistant	☐ To be fed grapes	☐ Utter devotion
☐ Hot coffee	☐ A cup of tea	☐ A stiff one	☐ Cupcakes
☐ A hot bath	☐ Therapy	☐ Mother's little helper	☐ Thermostat control
☐ A cold shower	☐ A good night's sleep	☐ A pep talk	☐ A cold drink
☐ Some good gossip	☐ Jewelry	☐ Fewer interruptions	☐ Inner peace
☐ A day in pajamas	☐ To be the center of attention	☐ To win	☐ A day without poop
☐ A day out of sweats	☐ To sit down for a minute	☐ A sugar fix	☐ Sympathy
☐ New shoes	☐ A happy child	☐ Well-behaved inner child	☐ Empathy
☐ A bit of effort	☐ A happy spouse	☐ Well-behaved children	☐ A comfy chair
☐ Barf-free clothing	☐ Praise for my intellect	☐ To get outside	☐ Second helping of dessert
☐ Stress relief	☐ Deodorant	☐ A guilty pleasure	☐ A brisk walk
☐ Family dinner	☐ An apology	☐ A primal scream	☐ A "Please"
☐ Beds all made	☐ Lottery win	☐ A clean kitchen	☐ A "Thank you"
☐ A pick-me-up	☐ A six-pack	☐ More chocolate	☐ A present
☐ Fireman fantasy	☐ Dust bunny eradication	☐ A foot rub	☐ My prince to come
☐ The toothpaste capped	☐ A parking spot	☐ Chores completed	☐ A big bowl of ice cream
☐ A good hair day	☐ No tears	☐ Snuggle time	☐ A serenade
☐ Less laundry	☐ Stain-free day	☐ A good laugh	☐ Grace under pressure
☐ Window-shopping	☐ A haiku	☐ Clean sheets	☐ Mind over matter
☐ Complete obedience	☐ Cuddling	☐ A glass of bubbly	☐ Good will
☐ A chuckle	☐ Coddling	☐ Better neighbors	☐ Flowers
☐ Clean children	☐ A blowout	☐ To hear I'm cool	☐ A miracle
☐ A sincere compliment	☐ An empty dishwasher	☐ To hear I'm hot	☐ Some "me" time
☐ Mani-pedi	☐ You to put on a sweater	☐ Yoga	☐ A good cry
☐ A shoulder to cry on	☐ A nap	☐ Validation	☐ Girl's night out
☐ A random thoughtful act	☐ More help	☐ Breakfast in bed	☐ Romantic dinner
☐ To feel like a million bucks	☐ Complete silence	☐ Control of remote	☐ Full-time help
☐ To look like a million bucks	☐ Extra cheese	☐ A neck rub	☐ Just a little appreciation
☐ A million bucks	☐ A bra that fits	☐ A big smile	☐ Just you

☐ **PLEASE**   ☐ **PRETTY PLEASE**   ☐ **THANK YOU**   ☐ **OR ELSE**

	MONTH	DAY	YEAR
SIGNATURE (ACTUAL NAME OF MOTHER)			

"IS IT REALLY SO MUCH TO ASK?"

THINGS MOM REALLY, REALLY, REALLY NEEDS

☐ **SOON** ☐ **TODAY** ☐ **RIGHT NOW** ☐ **FROM NOW ON**

SOON	TODAY	RIGHT NOW	FROM NOW ON
☐ A break	☐ For you to read my mind	☐ Candlelight	☐ Movie night
☐ Less whine	☐ An aspirin	☐ Space	☐ A side of fries
☐ More wine	☐ Some respect	☐ A well-stocked fridge	☐ Some lovin'
☐ Your love	☐ Pizza, toppings my choice	☐ Commiseration	☐ A chauffeur
☐ Chocolate	☐ A good book	☐ To sleep in	☐ Inside voices
☐ A vacation	☐ Work-life balance	☐ A margarita	☐ A little more help
☐ Peace	☐ For you to make dinner	☐ Tantrum absence	☐ Vim
☐ Quiet	☐ A little enthusiasm	☐ The toilet seat down	☐ Vigor
☐ Peace and quiet	☐ To recapture my youth	☐ Someone to take out dog	☐ A good babysitter
☐ A date night	☐ Alone time	☐ Someone to bring in cat	☐ Soft lights
☐ The toilet paper replaced	☐ Alone time in bathroom	☐ A makeover	☐ Soft music
☐ Pampering	☐ Someone to admit I'm right	☐ Costume drama on DVR	☐ Clean clothes
☐ A kiss	☐ A shopping spree	☐ Reality TV on DVR	☐ Time to read
☐ A hug	☐ Attitude of gratitude	☐ Punctuality	☐ A day without dieting
☐ A bear hug	☐ Pie	☐ Endorphin rush	☐ Calm
☐ Someone to listen	☐ A massage	☐ Personal shopper	☐ A friendly phone call
☐ Takeout	☐ An ego massage	☐ Personal schlepper	☐ A day off
☐ A little help	☐ All the answers	☐ A mate to that sock	☐ A smidgen of kindness
☐ To fit into those jeans	☐ Any answer	☐ Time to reflect	☐ A good workout
☐ Privacy	☐ Sweet nothings	☐ A little consideration	☐ A new job
☐ A love note	☐ Personal trainer	☐ Spa day	☐ Even more wine
☐ No complaints	☐ Personal assistant	☐ To be fed grapes	☐ Utter devotion
☐ Hot coffee	☐ A cup of tea	☐ A stiff one	☐ Cupcakes
☐ A hot bath	☐ Therapy	☐ Mother's little helper	☐ Thermostat control
☐ A cold shower	☐ A good night's sleep	☐ A pep talk	☐ A cold drink
☐ Some good gossip	☐ Jewelry	☐ Fewer interruptions	☐ Inner peace
☐ A day in pajamas	☐ To be the center of attention	☐ To win	☐ A day without poop
☐ A day out of sweats	☐ To sit down for a minute	☐ A sugar fix	☐ Sympathy
☐ New shoes	☐ A happy child	☐ Well-behaved inner child	☐ Empathy
☐ A bit of effort	☐ A happy spouse	☐ Well-behaved children	☐ A comfy chair
☐ Barf-free clothing	☐ Praise for my intellect	☐ To get outside	☐ Second helping of dessert
☐ Stress relief	☐ Deodorant	☐ A guilty pleasure	☐ A brisk walk
☐ Family dinner	☐ An apology	☐ A primal scream	☐ A "Please"
☐ Beds all made	☐ Lottery win	☐ A clean kitchen	☐ A "Thank you"
☐ A pick-me-up	☐ A six-pack	☐ More chocolate	☐ A present
☐ Fireman fantasy	☐ Dust bunny eradication	☐ A foot rub	☐ My prince to come
☐ The toothpaste capped	☐ A parking spot	☐ Chores completed	☐ A big bowl of ice cream
☐ A good hair day	☐ No tears	☐ Snuggle time	☐ A serenade
☐ Less laundry	☐ Stain-free day	☐ A good laugh	☐ Grace under pressure
☐ Window-shopping	☐ A haiku	☐ Clean sheets	☐ Mind over matter
☐ Complete obedience	☐ Cuddling	☐ A glass of bubbly	☐ Good will
☐ A chuckle	☐ Coddling	☐ Better neighbors	☐ Flowers
☐ Clean children	☐ A blowout	☐ To hear I'm cool	☐ A miracle
☐ A sincere compliment	☐ An empty dishwasher	☐ To hear I'm hot	☐ Some "me" time
☐ Mani-pedi	☐ You to put on a sweater	☐ Yoga	☐ A good cry
☐ A shoulder to cry on	☐ A nap	☐ Validation	☐ Girl's night out
☐ A random thoughtful act	☐ More help	☐ Breakfast in bed	☐ Romantic dinner
☐ To feel like a million bucks	☐ Complete silence	☐ Control of remote	☐ Full-time help
☐ To look like a million bucks	☐ Extra cheese	☐ A neck rub	☐ Just a little appreciation
☐ A million bucks	☐ A bra that fits	☐ A big smile	☐ Just you

☐ **PLEASE** ☐ **PRETTY PLEASE** ☐ **THANK YOU** ☐ **OR ELSE**

SIGNATURE (ACTUAL NAME OF MOTHER)   MONTH   DAY   YEAR

"IS IT REALLY SO MUCH TO ASK?"

THINGS MOM REALLY, REALLY, REALLY NEEDS

☐ **SOON** ☐ **TODAY** ☐ **RIGHT NOW** ☐ **FROM NOW ON**

SOON	TODAY	RIGHT NOW	FROM NOW ON
☐ A break	☐ For you to read my mind	☐ Candlelight	☐ Movie night
☐ Less whine	☐ An aspirin	☐ Space	☐ A side of fries
☐ More wine	☐ Some respect	☐ A well-stocked fridge	☐ Some lovin'
☐ Your love	☐ Pizza, toppings my choice	☐ Commiseration	☐ A chauffeur
☐ Chocolate	☐ A good book	☐ To sleep in	☐ Inside voices
☐ A vacation	☐ Work-life balance	☐ A margarita	☐ A little more help
☐ Peace	☐ For you to make dinner	☐ Tantrum absence	☐ Vim
☐ Quiet	☐ A little enthusiasm	☐ The toilet seat down	☐ Vigor
☐ Peace and quiet	☐ To recapture my youth	☐ Someone to take out dog	☐ A good babysitter
☐ A date night	☐ Alone time	☐ Someone to bring in cat	☐ Soft lights
☐ The toilet paper replaced	☐ Alone time in bathroom	☐ A makeover	☐ Soft music
☐ Pampering	☐ Someone to admit I'm right	☐ Costume drama on DVR	☐ Clean clothes
☐ A kiss	☐ A shopping spree	☐ Reality TV on DVR	☐ Time to read
☐ A hug	☐ Attitude of gratitude	☐ Punctuality	☐ A day without dieting
☐ A bear hug	☐ Pie	☐ Endorphin rush	☐ Calm
☐ Someone to listen	☐ A massage	☐ Personal shopper	☐ A friendly phone call
☐ Takeout	☐ An ego massage	☐ Personal schlepper	☐ A day off
☐ A little help	☐ All the answers	☐ A mate to that sock	☐ A smidgen of kindness
☐ To fit into those jeans	☐ Any answer	☐ Time to reflect	☐ A good workout
☐ Privacy	☐ Sweet nothings	☐ A little consideration	☐ A new job
☐ A love note	☐ Personal trainer	☐ Spa day	☐ Even more wine
☐ No complaints	☐ Personal assistant	☐ To be fed grapes	☐ Utter devotion
☐ Hot coffee	☐ A cup of tea	☐ A stiff one	☐ Cupcakes
☐ A hot bath	☐ Therapy	☐ Mother's little helper	☐ Thermostat control
☐ A cold shower	☐ A good night's sleep	☐ A pep talk	☐ A cold drink
☐ Some good gossip	☐ Jewelry	☐ Fewer interruptions	☐ Inner peace
☐ A day in pajamas	☐ To be the center of attention	☐ To win	☐ A day without poop
☐ A day out of sweats	☐ To sit down for a minute	☐ A sugar fix	☐ Sympathy
☐ New shoes	☐ A happy child	☐ Well-behaved inner child	☐ Empathy
☐ A bit of effort	☐ A happy spouse	☐ Well-behaved children	☐ A comfy chair
☐ Barf-free clothing	☐ Praise for my intellect	☐ To get outside	☐ Second helping of dessert
☐ Stress relief	☐ Deodorant	☐ A guilty pleasure	☐ A brisk walk
☐ Family dinner	☐ An apology	☐ A primal scream	☐ A "Please"
☐ Beds all made	☐ Lottery win	☐ A clean kitchen	☐ A "Thank you"
☐ A pick-me-up	☐ A six-pack	☐ More chocolate	☐ A present
☐ Fireman fantasy	☐ Dust bunny eradication	☐ A foot rub	☐ My prince to come
☐ The toothpaste capped	☐ A parking spot	☐ Chores completed	☐ A big bowl of ice cream
☐ A good hair day	☐ No tears	☐ Snuggle time	☐ A serenade
☐ Less laundry	☐ Stain-free day	☐ A good laugh	☐ Grace under pressure
☐ Window-shopping	☐ A haiku	☐ Clean sheets	☐ Mind over matter
☐ Complete obedience	☐ Cuddling	☐ A glass of bubbly	☐ Good will
☐ A chuckle	☐ Coddling	☐ Better neighbors	☐ Flowers
☐ Clean children	☐ A blowout	☐ To hear I'm cool	☐ A miracle
☐ A sincere compliment	☐ An empty dishwasher	☐ To hear I'm hot	☐ Some "me" time
☐ Mani-pedi	☐ You to put on a sweater	☐ Yoga	☐ A good cry
☐ A shoulder to cry on	☐ A nap	☐ Validation	☐ Girl's night out
☐ A random thoughtful act	☐ More help	☐ Breakfast in bed	☐ Romantic dinner
☐ To feel like a million bucks	☐ Complete silence	☐ Control of remote	☐ Full-time help
☐ To look like a million bucks	☐ Extra cheese	☐ A neck rub	☐ Just a little appreciation
☐ A million bucks	☐ A bra that fits	☐ A big smile	☐ Just you

☐ **PLEASE** ☐ **PRETTY PLEASE** ☐ **THANK YOU** ☐ **OR ELSE**

SIGNATURE (ACTUAL NAME OF MOTHER) | MONTH | DAY | YEAR

"IS IT REALLY SO MUCH TO ASK?"

THINGS MOM REALLY, REALLY, REALLY NEEDS

☐ **SOON**   ☐ **TODAY**   ☐ **RIGHT NOW**   ☐ **FROM NOW ON**

SOON	TODAY	RIGHT NOW	FROM NOW ON
☐ A break	☐ For you to read my mind	☐ Candlelight	☐ Movie night
☐ Less whine	☐ An aspirin	☐ Space	☐ A side of fries
☐ More wine	☐ Some respect	☐ A well-stocked fridge	☐ Some lovin'
☐ Your love	☐ Pizza, toppings my choice	☐ Commiseration	☐ A chauffeur
☐ Chocolate	☐ A good book	☐ To sleep in	☐ Inside voices
☐ A vacation	☐ Work-life balance	☐ A margarita	☐ A little more help
☐ Peace	☐ For you to make dinner	☐ Tantrum absence	☐ Vim
☐ Quiet	☐ A little enthusiasm	☐ The toilet seat down	☐ Vigor
☐ Peace and quiet	☐ To recapture my youth	☐ Someone to take out dog	☐ A good babysitter
☐ A date night	☐ Alone time	☐ Someone to bring in cat	☐ Soft lights
☐ The toilet paper replaced	☐ Alone time in bathroom	☐ A makeover	☐ Soft music
☐ Pampering	☐ Someone to admit I'm right	☐ Costume drama on DVR	☐ Clean clothes
☐ A kiss	☐ A shopping spree	☐ Reality TV on DVR	☐ Time to read
☐ A hug	☐ Attitude of gratitude	☐ Punctuality	☐ A day without dieting
☐ A bear hug	☐ Pie	☐ Endorphin rush	☐ Calm
☐ Someone to listen	☐ A massage	☐ Personal shopper	☐ A friendly phone call
☐ Takeout	☐ An ego massage	☐ Personal schlepper	☐ A day off
☐ A little help	☐ All the answers	☐ A mate to that sock	☐ A smidgen of kindness
☐ To fit into those jeans	☐ Any answer	☐ Time to reflect	☐ A good workout
☐ Privacy	☐ Sweet nothings	☐ A little consideration	☐ A new job
☐ A love note	☐ Personal trainer	☐ Spa day	☐ Even more wine
☐ No complaints	☐ Personal assistant	☐ To be fed grapes	☐ Utter devotion
☐ Hot coffee	☐ A cup of tea	☐ A stiff one	☐ Cupcakes
☐ A hot bath	☐ Therapy	☐ Mother's little helper	☐ Thermostat control
☐ A cold shower	☐ A good night's sleep	☐ A pep talk	☐ A cold drink
☐ Some good gossip	☐ Jewelry	☐ Fewer interruptions	☐ Inner peace
☐ A day in pajamas	☐ To be the center of attention	☐ To win	☐ A day without poop
☐ A day out of sweats	☐ To sit down for a minute	☐ A sugar fix	☐ Sympathy
☐ New shoes	☐ A happy child	☐ Well-behaved inner child	☐ Empathy
☐ A bit of effort	☐ A happy spouse	☐ Well-behaved children	☐ A comfy chair
☐ Barf-free clothing	☐ Praise for my intellect	☐ To get outside	☐ Second helping of dessert
☐ Stress relief	☐ Deodorant	☐ A guilty pleasure	☐ A brisk walk
☐ Family dinner	☐ An apology	☐ A primal scream	☐ A "Please"
☐ Beds all made	☐ Lottery win	☐ A clean kitchen	☐ A "Thank you"
☐ A pick-me-up	☐ A six-pack	☐ More chocolate	☐ A present
☐ Fireman fantasy	☐ Dust bunny eradication	☐ A foot rub	☐ My prince to come
☐ The toothpaste capped	☐ A parking spot	☐ Chores completed	☐ A big bowl of ice cream
☐ A good hair day	☐ No tears	☐ Snuggle time	☐ A serenade
☐ Less laundry	☐ Stain-free day	☐ A good laugh	☐ Grace under pressure
☐ Window-shopping	☐ A haiku	☐ Clean sheets	☐ Mind over matter
☐ Complete obedience	☐ Cuddling	☐ A glass of bubbly	☐ Good will
☐ A chuckle	☐ Coddling	☐ Better neighbors	☐ Flowers
☐ Clean children	☐ A blowout	☐ To hear I'm cool	☐ A miracle
☐ A sincere compliment	☐ An empty dishwasher	☐ To hear I'm hot	☐ Some "me" time
☐ Mani-pedi	☐ You to put on a sweater	☐ Yoga	☐ A good cry
☐ A shoulder to cry on	☐ A nap	☐ Validation	☐ Girl's night out
☐ A random thoughtful act	☐ More help	☐ Breakfast in bed	☐ Romantic dinner
☐ To feel like a million bucks	☐ Complete silence	☐ Control of remote	☐ Full-time help
☐ To look like a million bucks	☐ Extra cheese	☐ A neck rub	☐ Just a little appreciation
☐ A million bucks	☐ A bra that fits	☐ A big smile	☐ Just you

☐ **PLEASE**   ☐ **PRETTY PLEASE**   ☐ **THANK YOU**   ☐ **OR ELSE**

SIGNATURE (ACTUAL NAME OF MOTHER)   MONTH   DAY   YEAR

"IS IT REALLY SO MUCH TO ASK?"

THINGS MOM REALLY, REALLY, REALLY NEEDS

☐ **SOON**   ☐ **TODAY**   ☐ **RIGHT NOW**   ☐ **FROM NOW ON**

SOON	TODAY	RIGHT NOW	FROM NOW ON
☐ A break	☐ For you to read my mind	☐ Candlelight	☐ Movie night
☐ Less whine	☐ An aspirin	☐ Space	☐ A side of fries
☐ More wine	☐ Some respect	☐ A well-stocked fridge	☐ Some lovin'
☐ Your love	☐ Pizza, toppings my choice	☐ Commiseration	☐ A chauffeur
☐ Chocolate	☐ A good book	☐ To sleep in	☐ Inside voices
☐ A vacation	☐ Work-life balance	☐ A margarita	☐ A little more help
☐ Peace	☐ For you to make dinner	☐ Tantrum absence	☐ Vim
☐ Quiet	☐ A little enthusiasm	☐ The toilet seat down	☐ Vigor
☐ Peace and quiet	☐ To recapture my youth	☐ Someone to take out dog	☐ A good babysitter
☐ A date night	☐ Alone time	☐ Someone to bring in cat	☐ Soft lights
☐ The toilet paper replaced	☐ Alone time in bathroom	☐ A makeover	☐ Soft music
☐ Pampering	☐ Someone to admit I'm right	☐ Costume drama on DVR	☐ Clean clothes
☐ A kiss	☐ A shopping spree	☐ Reality TV on DVR	☐ Time to read
☐ A hug	☐ Attitude of gratitude	☐ Punctuality	☐ A day without dieting
☐ A bear hug	☐ Pie	☐ Endorphin rush	☐ Calm
☐ Someone to listen	☐ A massage	☐ Personal shopper	☐ A friendly phone call
☐ Takeout	☐ An ego massage	☐ Personal schlepper	☐ A day off
☐ A little help	☐ All the answers	☐ A mate to that sock	☐ A smidgen of kindness
☐ To fit into those jeans	☐ Any answer	☐ Time to reflect	☐ A good workout
☐ Privacy	☐ Sweet nothings	☐ A little consideration	☐ A new job
☐ A love note	☐ Personal trainer	☐ Spa day	☐ Even more wine
☐ No complaints	☐ Personal assistant	☐ To be fed grapes	☐ Utter devotion
☐ Hot coffee	☐ A cup of tea	☐ A stiff one	☐ Cupcakes
☐ A hot bath	☐ Therapy	☐ Mother's little helper	☐ Thermostat control
☐ A cold shower	☐ A good night's sleep	☐ A pep talk	☐ A cold drink
☐ Some good gossip	☐ Jewelry	☐ Fewer interruptions	☐ Inner peace
☐ A day in pajamas	☐ To be the center of attention	☐ To win	☐ A day without poop
☐ A day out of sweats	☐ To sit down for a minute	☐ A sugar fix	☐ Sympathy
☐ New shoes	☐ A happy child	☐ Well-behaved inner child	☐ Empathy
☐ A bit of effort	☐ A happy spouse	☐ Well-behaved children	☐ A comfy chair
☐ Barf-free clothing	☐ Praise for my intellect	☐ To get outside	☐ Second helping of dessert
☐ Stress relief	☐ Deodorant	☐ A guilty pleasure	☐ A brisk walk
☐ Family dinner	☐ An apology	☐ A primal scream	☐ A "Please"
☐ Beds all made	☐ Lottery win	☐ A clean kitchen	☐ A "Thank you"
☐ A pick-me-up	☐ A six-pack	☐ More chocolate	☐ A present
☐ Fireman fantasy	☐ Dust bunny eradication	☐ A foot rub	☐ My prince to come
☐ The toothpaste capped	☐ A parking spot	☐ Chores completed	☐ A big bowl of ice cream
☐ A good hair day	☐ No tears	☐ Snuggle time	☐ A serenade
☐ Less laundry	☐ Stain-free day	☐ A good laugh	☐ Grace under pressure
☐ Window-shopping	☐ A haiku	☐ Clean sheets	☐ Mind over matter
☐ Complete obedience	☐ Cuddling	☐ A glass of bubbly	☐ Good will
☐ A chuckle	☐ Coddling	☐ Better neighbors	☐ Flowers
☐ Clean children	☐ A blowout	☐ To hear I'm cool	☐ A miracle
☐ A sincere compliment	☐ An empty dishwasher	☐ To hear I'm hot	☐ Some "me" time
☐ Mani-pedi	☐ You to put on a sweater	☐ Yoga	☐ A good cry
☐ A shoulder to cry on	☐ A nap	☐ Validation	☐ Girl's night out
☐ A random thoughtful act	☐ More help	☐ Breakfast in bed	☐ Romantic dinner
☐ To feel like a million bucks	☐ Complete silence	☐ Control of remote	☐ Full-time help
☐ To look like a million bucks	☐ Extra cheese	☐ A neck rub	☐ Just a little appreciation
☐ A million bucks	☐ A bra that fits	☐ A big smile	☐ Just you

☐ **PLEASE**   ☐ **PRETTY PLEASE**   ☐ **THANK YOU**   ☐ **OR ELSE**

	MONTH	DAY	YEAR
SIGNATURE (ACTUAL NAME OF MOTHER)			

"IS IT REALLY SO MUCH TO ASK?"

THINGS MOM REALLY, REALLY, REALLY NEEDS

☐ **SOON**   ☐ **TODAY**   ☐ **RIGHT NOW**   ☐ **FROM NOW ON**

☐ A break	☐ For you to read my mind	☐ Candlelight	☐ Movie night
☐ Less whine	☐ An aspirin	☐ Space	☐ A side of fries
☐ More wine	☐ Some respect	☐ A well-stocked fridge	☐ Some lovin'
☐ Your love	☐ Pizza, toppings my choice	☐ Commiseration	☐ A chauffeur
☐ Chocolate	☐ A good book	☐ To sleep in	☐ Inside voices
☐ A vacation	☐ Work-life balance	☐ A margarita	☐ A little more help
☐ Peace	☐ For you to make dinner	☐ Tantrum absence	☐ Vim
☐ Quiet	☐ A little enthusiasm	☐ The toilet seat down	☐ Vigor
☐ Peace and quiet	☐ To recapture my youth	☐ Someone to take out dog	☐ A good babysitter
☐ A date night	☐ Alone time	☐ Someone to bring in cat	☐ Soft lights
☐ The toilet paper replaced	☐ Alone time in bathroom	☐ A makeover	☐ Soft music
☐ Pampering	☐ Someone to admit I'm right	☐ Costume drama on DVR	☐ Clean clothes
☐ A kiss	☐ A shopping spree	☐ Reality TV on DVR	☐ Time to read
☐ A hug	☐ Attitude of gratitude	☐ Punctuality	☐ A day without dieting
☐ A bear hug	☐ Pie	☐ Endorphin rush	☐ Calm
☐ Someone to listen	☐ A massage	☐ Personal shopper	☐ A friendly phone call
☐ Takeout	☐ An ego massage	☐ Personal schlepper	☐ A day off
☐ A little help	☐ All the answers	☐ A mate to that sock	☐ A smidgen of kindness
☐ To fit into those jeans	☐ Any answer	☐ Time to reflect	☐ A good workout
☐ Privacy	☐ Sweet nothings	☐ A little consideration	☐ A new job
☐ A love note	☐ Personal trainer	☐ Spa day	☐ Even more wine
☐ No complaints	☐ Personal assistant	☐ To be fed grapes	☐ Utter devotion
☐ Hot coffee	☐ A cup of tea	☐ A stiff one	☐ Cupcakes
☐ A hot bath	☐ Therapy	☐ Mother's little helper	☐ Thermostat control
☐ A cold shower	☐ A good night's sleep	☐ A pep talk	☐ A cold drink
☐ Some good gossip	☐ Jewelry	☐ Fewer interruptions	☐ Inner peace
☐ A day in pajamas	☐ To be the center of attention	☐ To win	☐ A day without poop
☐ A day out of sweats	☐ To sit down for a minute	☐ A sugar fix	☐ Sympathy
☐ New shoes	☐ A happy child	☐ Well-behaved inner child	☐ Empathy
☐ A bit of effort	☐ A happy spouse	☐ Well-behaved children	☐ A comfy chair
☐ Barf-free clothing	☐ Praise for my intellect	☐ To get outside	☐ Second helping of dessert
☐ Stress relief	☐ Deodorant	☐ A guilty pleasure	☐ A brisk walk
☐ Family dinner	☐ An apology	☐ A primal scream	☐ A "Please"
☐ Beds all made	☐ Lottery win	☐ A clean kitchen	☐ A "Thank you"
☐ A pick-me-up	☐ A six-pack	☐ More chocolate	☐ A present
☐ Fireman fantasy	☐ Dust bunny eradication	☐ A foot rub	☐ My prince to come
☐ The toothpaste capped	☐ A parking spot	☐ Chores completed	☐ A big bowl of ice cream
☐ A good hair day	☐ No tears	☐ Snuggle time	☐ A serenade
☐ Less laundry	☐ Stain-free day	☐ A good laugh	☐ Grace under pressure
☐ Window-shopping	☐ A haiku	☐ Clean sheets	☐ Mind over matter
☐ Complete obedience	☐ Cuddling	☐ A glass of bubbly	☐ Good will
☐ A chuckle	☐ Coddling	☐ Better neighbors	☐ Flowers
☐ Clean children	☐ A blowout	☐ To hear I'm cool	☐ A miracle
☐ A sincere compliment	☐ An empty dishwasher	☐ To hear I'm hot	☐ Some "me" time
☐ Mani-pedi	☐ You to put on a sweater	☐ Yoga	☐ A good cry
☐ A shoulder to cry on	☐ A nap	☐ Validation	☐ Girl's night out
☐ A random thoughtful act	☐ More help	☐ Breakfast in bed	☐ Romantic dinner
☐ To feel like a million bucks	☐ Complete silence	☐ Control of remote	☐ Full-time help
☐ To look like a million bucks	☐ Extra cheese	☐ A neck rub	☐ Just a little appreciation
☐ A million bucks	☐ A bra that fits	☐ A big smile	☐ Just you

☐ **PLEASE**   ☐ **PRETTY PLEASE**   ☐ **THANK YOU**   ☐ **OR ELSE**

SIGNATURE (ACTUAL NAME OF MOTHER) | MONTH | DAY | YEAR

"IS IT REALLY SO MUCH TO ASK?"

THINGS MOM REALLY, REALLY, REALLY NEEDS

☐ **SOON**   ☐ **TODAY**   ☐ **RIGHT NOW**   ☐ **FROM NOW ON**

☐ A break	☐ For you to read my mind	☐ Candlelight	☐ Movie night
☐ Less whine	☐ An aspirin	☐ Space	☐ A side of fries
☐ More wine	☐ Some respect	☐ A well-stocked fridge	☐ Some lovin'
☐ Your love	☐ Pizza, toppings my choice	☐ Commiseration	☐ A chauffeur
☐ Chocolate	☐ A good book	☐ To sleep in	☐ Inside voices
☐ A vacation	☐ Work-life balance	☐ A margarita	☐ A little more help
☐ Peace	☐ For you to make dinner	☐ Tantrum absence	☐ Vim
☐ Quiet	☐ A little enthusiasm	☐ The toilet seat down	☐ Vigor
☐ Peace and quiet	☐ To recapture my youth	☐ Someone to take out dog	☐ A good babysitter
☐ A date night	☐ Alone time	☐ Someone to bring in cat	☐ Soft lights
☐ The toilet paper replaced	☐ Alone time in bathroom	☐ A makeover	☐ Soft music
☐ Pampering	☐ Someone to admit I'm right	☐ Costume drama on DVR	☐ Clean clothes
☐ A kiss	☐ A shopping spree	☐ Reality TV on DVR	☐ Time to read
☐ A hug	☐ Attitude of gratitude	☐ Punctuality	☐ A day without dieting
☐ A bear hug	☐ Pie	☐ Endorphin rush	☐ Calm
☐ Someone to listen	☐ A massage	☐ Personal shopper	☐ A friendly phone call
☐ Takeout	☐ An ego massage	☐ Personal schlepper	☐ A day off
☐ A little help	☐ All the answers	☐ A mate to that sock	☐ A smidgen of kindness
☐ To fit into those jeans	☐ Any answer	☐ Time to reflect	☐ A good workout
☐ Privacy	☐ Sweet nothings	☐ A little consideration	☐ A new job
☐ A love note	☐ Personal trainer	☐ Spa day	☐ Even more wine
☐ No complaints	☐ Personal assistant	☐ To be fed grapes	☐ Utter devotion
☐ Hot coffee	☐ A cup of tea	☐ A stiff one	☐ Cupcakes
☐ A hot bath	☐ Therapy	☐ Mother's little helper	☐ Thermostat control
☐ A cold shower	☐ A good night's sleep	☐ A pep talk	☐ A cold drink
☐ Some good gossip	☐ Jewelry	☐ Fewer interruptions	☐ Inner peace
☐ A day in pajamas	☐ To be the center of attention	☐ To win	☐ A day without poop
☐ A day out of sweats	☐ To sit down for a minute	☐ A sugar fix	☐ Sympathy
☐ New shoes	☐ A happy child	☐ Well-behaved inner child	☐ Empathy
☐ A bit of effort	☐ A happy spouse	☐ Well-behaved children	☐ A comfy chair
☐ Barf-free clothing	☐ Praise for my intellect	☐ To get outside	☐ Second helping of dessert
☐ Stress relief	☐ Deodorant	☐ A guilty pleasure	☐ A brisk walk
☐ Family dinner	☐ An apology	☐ A primal scream	☐ A "Please"
☐ Beds all made	☐ Lottery win	☐ A clean kitchen	☐ A "Thank you"
☐ A pick-me-up	☐ A six-pack	☐ More chocolate	☐ A present
☐ Fireman fantasy	☐ Dust bunny eradication	☐ A foot rub	☐ My prince to come
☐ The toothpaste capped	☐ A parking spot	☐ Chores completed	☐ A big bowl of ice cream
☐ A good hair day	☐ No tears	☐ Snuggle time	☐ A serenade
☐ Less laundry	☐ Stain-free day	☐ A good laugh	☐ Grace under pressure
☐ Window-shopping	☐ A haiku	☐ Clean sheets	☐ Mind over matter
☐ Complete obedience	☐ Cuddling	☐ A glass of bubbly	☐ Good will
☐ A chuckle	☐ Coddling	☐ Better neighbors	☐ Flowers
☐ Clean children	☐ A blowout	☐ To hear I'm cool	☐ A miracle
☐ A sincere compliment	☐ An empty dishwasher	☐ To hear I'm hot	☐ Some "me" time
☐ Mani-pedi	☐ You to put on a sweater	☐ Yoga	☐ A good cry
☐ A shoulder to cry on	☐ A nap	☐ Validation	☐ Girl's night out
☐ A random thoughtful act	☐ More help	☐ Breakfast in bed	☐ Romantic dinner
☐ To feel like a million bucks	☐ Complete silence	☐ Control of remote	☐ Full-time help
☐ To look like a million bucks	☐ Extra cheese	☐ A neck rub	☐ Just a little appreciation
☐ A million bucks	☐ A bra that fits	☐ A big smile	☐ Just you

☐ **PLEASE**   ☐ **PRETTY PLEASE**   ☐ **THANK YOU**   ☐ **OR ELSE**

SIGNATURE (ACTUAL NAME OF MOTHER)		MONTH	DAY	YEAR

"IS IT REALLY SO MUCH TO ASK?"

THINGS MOM REALLY, REALLY, REALLY NEEDS

☐ **SOON**   ☐ **TODAY**   ☐ **RIGHT NOW**   ☐ **FROM NOW ON**

SOON	TODAY	RIGHT NOW	FROM NOW ON
☐ A break	☐ For you to read my mind	☐ Candlelight	☐ Movie night
☐ Less whine	☐ An aspirin	☐ Space	☐ A side of fries
☐ More wine	☐ Some respect	☐ A well-stocked fridge	☐ Some lovin'
☐ Your love	☐ Pizza, toppings my choice	☐ Commiseration	☐ A chauffeur
☐ Chocolate	☐ A good book	☐ To sleep in	☐ Inside voices
☐ A vacation	☐ Work-life balance	☐ A margarita	☐ A little more help
☐ Peace	☐ For you to make dinner	☐ Tantrum absence	☐ Vim
☐ Quiet	☐ A little enthusiasm	☐ The toilet seat down	☐ Vigor
☐ Peace and quiet	☐ To recapture my youth	☐ Someone to take out dog	☐ A good babysitter
☐ A date night	☐ Alone time	☐ Someone to bring in cat	☐ Soft lights
☐ The toilet paper replaced	☐ Alone time in bathroom	☐ A makeover	☐ Soft music
☐ Pampering	☐ Someone to admit I'm right	☐ Costume drama on DVR	☐ Clean clothes
☐ A kiss	☐ A shopping spree	☐ Reality TV on DVR	☐ Time to read
☐ A hug	☐ Attitude of gratitude	☐ Punctuality	☐ A day without dieting
☐ A bear hug	☐ Pie	☐ Endorphin rush	☐ Calm
☐ Someone to listen	☐ A massage	☐ Personal shopper	☐ A friendly phone call
☐ Takeout	☐ An ego massage	☐ Personal schlepper	☐ A day off
☐ A little help	☐ All the answers	☐ A mate to that sock	☐ A smidgen of kindness
☐ To fit into those jeans	☐ Any answer	☐ Time to reflect	☐ A good workout
☐ Privacy	☐ Sweet nothings	☐ A little consideration	☐ A new job
☐ A love note	☐ Personal trainer	☐ Spa day	☐ Even more wine
☐ No complaints	☐ Personal assistant	☐ To be fed grapes	☐ Utter devotion
☐ Hot coffee	☐ A cup of tea	☐ A stiff one	☐ Cupcakes
☐ A hot bath	☐ Therapy	☐ Mother's little helper	☐ Thermostat control
☐ A cold shower	☐ A good night's sleep	☐ A pep talk	☐ A cold drink
☐ Some good gossip	☐ Jewelry	☐ Fewer interruptions	☐ Inner peace
☐ A day in pajamas	☐ To be the center of attention	☐ To win	☐ A day without poop
☐ A day out of sweats	☐ To sit down for a minute	☐ A sugar fix	☐ Sympathy
☐ New shoes	☐ A happy child	☐ Well-behaved inner child	☐ Empathy
☐ A bit of effort	☐ A happy spouse	☐ Well-behaved children	☐ A comfy chair
☐ Barf-free clothing	☐ Praise for my intellect	☐ To get outside	☐ Second helping of dessert
☐ Stress relief	☐ Deodorant	☐ A guilty pleasure	☐ A brisk walk
☐ Family dinner	☐ An apology	☐ A primal scream	☐ A "Please"
☐ Beds all made	☐ Lottery win	☐ A clean kitchen	☐ A "Thank you"
☐ A pick-me-up	☐ A six-pack	☐ More chocolate	☐ A present
☐ Fireman fantasy	☐ Dust bunny eradication	☐ A foot rub	☐ My prince to come
☐ The toothpaste capped	☐ A parking spot	☐ Chores completed	☐ A big bowl of ice cream
☐ A good hair day	☐ No tears	☐ Snuggle time	☐ A serenade
☐ Less laundry	☐ Stain-free day	☐ A good laugh	☐ Grace under pressure
☐ Window-shopping	☐ A haiku	☐ Clean sheets	☐ Mind over matter
☐ Complete obedience	☐ Cuddling	☐ A glass of bubbly	☐ Good will
☐ A chuckle	☐ Coddling	☐ Better neighbors	☐ Flowers
☐ Clean children	☐ A blowout	☐ To hear I'm cool	☐ A miracle
☐ A sincere compliment	☐ An empty dishwasher	☐ To hear I'm hot	☐ Some "me" time
☐ Mani-pedi	☐ You to put on a sweater	☐ Yoga	☐ A good cry
☐ A shoulder to cry on	☐ A nap	☐ Validation	☐ Girl's night out
☐ A random thoughtful act	☐ More help	☐ Breakfast in bed	☐ Romantic dinner
☐ To feel like a million bucks	☐ Complete silence	☐ Control of remote	☐ Full-time help
☐ To look like a million bucks	☐ Extra cheese	☐ A neck rub	☐ Just a little appreciation
☐ A million bucks	☐ A bra that fits	☐ A big smile	☐ Just you

☐ **PLEASE**   ☐ **PRETTY PLEASE**   ☐ **THANK YOU**   ☐ **OR ELSE**

SIGNATURE (ACTUAL NAME OF MOTHER)   MONTH : DAY : YEAR

"IS IT REALLY SO MUCH TO ASK?"

THINGS MOM REALLY, REALLY, REALLY NEEDS

☐ **SOON**   ☐ **TODAY**   ☐ **RIGHT NOW**   ☐ **FROM NOW ON**

SOON	TODAY	RIGHT NOW	FROM NOW ON
☐ A break	☐ For you to read my mind	☐ Candlelight	☐ Movie night
☐ Less whine	☐ An aspirin	☐ Space	☐ A side of fries
☐ More wine	☐ Some respect	☐ A well-stocked fridge	☐ Some lovin'
☐ Your love	☐ Pizza, toppings my choice	☐ Commiseration	☐ A chauffeur
☐ Chocolate	☐ A good book	☐ To sleep in	☐ Inside voices
☐ A vacation	☐ Work-life balance	☐ A margarita	☐ A little more help
☐ Peace	☐ For you to make dinner	☐ Tantrum absence	☐ Vim
☐ Quiet	☐ A little enthusiasm	☐ The toilet seat down	☐ Vigor
☐ Peace and quiet	☐ To recapture my youth	☐ Someone to take out dog	☐ A good babysitter
☐ A date night	☐ Alone time	☐ Someone to bring in cat	☐ Soft lights
☐ The toilet paper replaced	☐ Alone time in bathroom	☐ A makeover	☐ Soft music
☐ Pampering	☐ Someone to admit I'm right	☐ Costume drama on DVR	☐ Clean clothes
☐ A kiss	☐ A shopping spree	☐ Reality TV on DVR	☐ Time to read
☐ A hug	☐ Attitude of gratitude	☐ Punctuality	☐ A day without dieting
☐ A bear hug	☐ Pie	☐ Endorphin rush	☐ Calm
☐ Someone to listen	☐ A massage	☐ Personal shopper	☐ A friendly phone call
☐ Takeout	☐ An ego massage	☐ Personal schlepper	☐ A day off
☐ A little help	☐ All the answers	☐ A mate to that sock	☐ A smidgen of kindness
☐ To fit into those jeans	☐ Any answer	☐ Time to reflect	☐ A good workout
☐ Privacy	☐ Sweet nothings	☐ A little consideration	☐ A new job
☐ A love note	☐ Personal trainer	☐ Spa day	☐ Even more wine
☐ No complaints	☐ Personal assistant	☐ To be fed grapes	☐ Utter devotion
☐ Hot coffee	☐ A cup of tea	☐ A stiff one	☐ Cupcakes
☐ A hot bath	☐ Therapy	☐ Mother's little helper	☐ Thermostat control
☐ A cold shower	☐ A good night's sleep	☐ A pep talk	☐ A cold drink
☐ Some good gossip	☐ Jewelry	☐ Fewer interruptions	☐ Inner peace
☐ A day in pajamas	☐ To be the center of attention	☐ To win	☐ A day without poop
☐ A day out of sweats	☐ To sit down for a minute	☐ A sugar fix	☐ Sympathy
☐ New shoes	☐ A happy child	☐ Well-behaved inner child	☐ Empathy
☐ A bit of effort	☐ A happy spouse	☐ Well-behaved children	☐ A comfy chair
☐ Barf-free clothing	☐ Praise for my intellect	☐ To get outside	☐ Second helping of dessert
☐ Stress relief	☐ Deodorant	☐ A guilty pleasure	☐ A brisk walk
☐ Family dinner	☐ An apology	☐ A primal scream	☐ A "Please"
☐ Beds all made	☐ Lottery win	☐ A clean kitchen	☐ A "Thank you"
☐ A pick-me-up	☐ A six-pack	☐ More chocolate	☐ A present
☐ Fireman fantasy	☐ Dust bunny eradication	☐ A foot rub	☐ My prince to come
☐ The toothpaste capped	☐ A parking spot	☐ Chores completed	☐ A big bowl of ice cream
☐ A good hair day	☐ No tears	☐ Snuggle time	☐ A serenade
☐ Less laundry	☐ Stain-free day	☐ A good laugh	☐ Grace under pressure
☐ Window-shopping	☐ A haiku	☐ Clean sheets	☐ Mind over matter
☐ Complete obedience	☐ Cuddling	☐ A glass of bubbly	☐ Good will
☐ A chuckle	☐ Coddling	☐ Better neighbors	☐ Flowers
☐ Clean children	☐ A blowout	☐ To hear I'm cool	☐ A miracle
☐ A sincere compliment	☐ An empty dishwasher	☐ To hear I'm hot	☐ Some "me" time
☐ Mani-pedi	☐ You to put on a sweater	☐ Yoga	☐ A good cry
☐ A shoulder to cry on	☐ A nap	☐ Validation	☐ Girl's night out
☐ A random thoughtful act	☐ More help	☐ Breakfast in bed	☐ Romantic dinner
☐ To feel like a million bucks	☐ Complete silence	☐ Control of remote	☐ Full-time help
☐ To look like a million bucks	☐ Extra cheese	☐ A neck rub	☐ Just a little appreciation
☐ A million bucks	☐ A bra that fits	☐ A big smile	☐ Just you

☐ **PLEASE**   ☐ **PRETTY PLEASE**   ☐ **THANK YOU**   ☐ **OR ELSE**

SIGNATURE (ACTUAL NAME OF MOTHER) | MONTH : DAY : YEAR

"IS IT REALLY SO MUCH TO ASK?"

THINGS MOM REALLY, REALLY, REALLY NEEDS

☐ **SOON**   ☐ **TODAY**   ☐ **RIGHT NOW**   ☐ **FROM NOW ON**

SOON	TODAY	RIGHT NOW	FROM NOW ON
☐ A break	☐ For you to read my mind	☐ Candlelight	☐ Movie night
☐ Less whine	☐ An aspirin	☐ Space	☐ A side of fries
☐ More wine	☐ Some respect	☐ A well-stocked fridge	☐ Some lovin'
☐ Your love	☐ Pizza, toppings my choice	☐ Commiseration	☐ A chauffeur
☐ Chocolate	☐ A good book	☐ To sleep in	☐ Inside voices
☐ A vacation	☐ Work-life balance	☐ A margarita	☐ A little more help
☐ Peace	☐ For you to make dinner	☐ Tantrum absence	☐ Vim
☐ Quiet	☐ A little enthusiasm	☐ The toilet seat down	☐ Vigor
☐ Peace and quiet	☐ To recapture my youth	☐ Someone to take out dog	☐ A good babysitter
☐ A date night	☐ Alone time	☐ Someone to bring in cat	☐ Soft lights
☐ The toilet paper replaced	☐ Alone time in bathroom	☐ A makeover	☐ Soft music
☐ Pampering	☐ Someone to admit I'm right	☐ Costume drama on DVR	☐ Clean clothes
☐ A kiss	☐ A shopping spree	☐ Reality TV on DVR	☐ Time to read
☐ A hug	☐ Attitude of gratitude	☐ Punctuality	☐ A day without dieting
☐ A bear hug	☐ Pie	☐ Endorphin rush	☐ Calm
☐ Someone to listen	☐ A massage	☐ Personal shopper	☐ A friendly phone call
☐ Takeout	☐ An ego massage	☐ Personal schlepper	☐ A day off
☐ A little help	☐ All the answers	☐ A mate to that sock	☐ A smidgen of kindness
☐ To fit into those jeans	☐ Any answer	☐ Time to reflect	☐ A good workout
☐ Privacy	☐ Sweet nothings	☐ A little consideration	☐ A new job
☐ A love note	☐ Personal trainer	☐ Spa day	☐ Even more wine
☐ No complaints	☐ Personal assistant	☐ To be fed grapes	☐ Utter devotion
☐ Hot coffee	☐ A cup of tea	☐ A stiff one	☐ Cupcakes
☐ A hot bath	☐ Therapy	☐ Mother's little helper	☐ Thermostat control
☐ A cold shower	☐ A good night's sleep	☐ A pep talk	☐ A cold drink
☐ Some good gossip	☐ Jewelry	☐ Fewer interruptions	☐ Inner peace
☐ A day in pajamas	☐ To be the center of attention	☐ To win	☐ A day without poop
☐ A day out of sweats	☐ To sit down for a minute	☐ A sugar fix	☐ Sympathy
☐ New shoes	☐ A happy child	☐ Well-behaved inner child	☐ Empathy
☐ A bit of effort	☐ A happy spouse	☐ Well-behaved children	☐ A comfy chair
☐ Barf-free clothing	☐ Praise for my intellect	☐ To get outside	☐ Second helping of dessert
☐ Stress relief	☐ Deodorant	☐ A guilty pleasure	☐ A brisk walk
☐ Family dinner	☐ An apology	☐ A primal scream	☐ A "Please"
☐ Beds all made	☐ Lottery win	☐ A clean kitchen	☐ A "Thank you"
☐ A pick-me-up	☐ A six-pack	☐ More chocolate	☐ A present
☐ Fireman fantasy	☐ Dust bunny eradication	☐ A foot rub	☐ My prince to come
☐ The toothpaste capped	☐ A parking spot	☐ Chores completed	☐ A big bowl of ice cream
☐ A good hair day	☐ No tears	☐ Snuggle time	☐ A serenade
☐ Less laundry	☐ Stain-free day	☐ A good laugh	☐ Grace under pressure
☐ Window-shopping	☐ A haiku	☐ Clean sheets	☐ Mind over matter
☐ Complete obedience	☐ Cuddling	☐ A glass of bubbly	☐ Good will
☐ A chuckle	☐ Coddling	☐ Better neighbors	☐ Flowers
☐ Clean children	☐ A blowout	☐ To hear I'm cool	☐ A miracle
☐ A sincere compliment	☐ An empty dishwasher	☐ To hear I'm hot	☐ Some "me" time
☐ Mani-pedi	☐ You to put on a sweater	☐ Yoga	☐ A good cry
☐ A shoulder to cry on	☐ A nap	☐ Validation	☐ Girl's night out
☐ A random thoughtful act	☐ More help	☐ Breakfast in bed	☐ Romantic dinner
☐ To feel like a million bucks	☐ Complete silence	☐ Control of remote	☐ Full-time help
☐ To look like a million bucks	☐ Extra cheese	☐ A neck rub	☐ Just a little appreciation
☐ A million bucks	☐ A bra that fits	☐ A big smile	☐ Just you

☐ **PLEASE**   ☐ **PRETTY PLEASE**   ☐ **THANK YOU**   ☐ **OR ELSE**

SIGNATURE (ACTUAL NAME OF MOTHER)

| MONTH | DAY | YEAR |

"IS IT REALLY SO MUCH TO ASK?"

THINGS MOM REALLY, REALLY, REALLY NEEDS

☐ **SOON** ☐ **TODAY** ☐ **RIGHT NOW** ☐ **FROM NOW ON**

SOON	TODAY	RIGHT NOW	FROM NOW ON
☐ A break	☐ For you to read my mind	☐ Candlelight	☐ Movie night
☐ Less whine	☐ An aspirin	☐ Space	☐ A side of fries
☐ More wine	☐ Some respect	☐ A well-stocked fridge	☐ Some lovin'
☐ Your love	☐ Pizza, toppings my choice	☐ Commiseration	☐ A chauffeur
☐ Chocolate	☐ A good book	☐ To sleep in	☐ Inside voices
☐ A vacation	☐ Work-life balance	☐ A margarita	☐ A little more help
☐ Peace	☐ For you to make dinner	☐ Tantrum absence	☐ Vim
☐ Quiet	☐ A little enthusiasm	☐ The toilet seat down	☐ Vigor
☐ Peace and quiet	☐ To recapture my youth	☐ Someone to take out dog	☐ A good babysitter
☐ A date night	☐ Alone time	☐ Someone to bring in cat	☐ Soft lights
☐ The toilet paper replaced	☐ Alone time in bathroom	☐ A makeover	☐ Soft music
☐ Pampering	☐ Someone to admit I'm right	☐ Costume drama on DVR	☐ Clean clothes
☐ A kiss	☐ A shopping spree	☐ Reality TV on DVR	☐ Time to read
☐ A hug	☐ Attitude of gratitude	☐ Punctuality	☐ A day without dieting
☐ A bear hug	☐ Pie	☐ Endorphin rush	☐ Calm
☐ Someone to listen	☐ A massage	☐ Personal shopper	☐ A friendly phone call
☐ Takeout	☐ An ego massage	☐ Personal schlepper	☐ A day off
☐ A little help	☐ All the answers	☐ A mate to that sock	☐ A smidgen of kindness
☐ To fit into those jeans	☐ Any answer	☐ Time to reflect	☐ A good workout
☐ Privacy	☐ Sweet nothings	☐ A little consideration	☐ A new job
☐ A love note	☐ Personal trainer	☐ Spa day	☐ Even more wine
☐ No complaints	☐ Personal assistant	☐ To be fed grapes	☐ Utter devotion
☐ Hot coffee	☐ A cup of tea	☐ A stiff one	☐ Cupcakes
☐ A hot bath	☐ Therapy	☐ Mother's little helper	☐ Thermostat control
☐ A cold shower	☐ A good night's sleep	☐ A pep talk	☐ A cold drink
☐ Some good gossip	☐ Jewelry	☐ Fewer interruptions	☐ Inner peace
☐ A day in pajamas	☐ To be the center of attention	☐ To win	☐ A day without poop
☐ A day out of sweats	☐ To sit down for a minute	☐ A sugar fix	☐ Sympathy
☐ New shoes	☐ A happy child	☐ Well-behaved inner child	☐ Empathy
☐ A bit of effort	☐ A happy spouse	☐ Well-behaved children	☐ A comfy chair
☐ Barf-free clothing	☐ Praise for my intellect	☐ To get outside	☐ Second helping of dessert
☐ Stress relief	☐ Deodorant	☐ A guilty pleasure	☐ A brisk walk
☐ Family dinner	☐ An apology	☐ A primal scream	☐ A "Please"
☐ Beds all made	☐ Lottery win	☐ A clean kitchen	☐ A "Thank you"
☐ A pick-me-up	☐ A six-pack	☐ More chocolate	☐ A present
☐ Fireman fantasy	☐ Dust bunny eradication	☐ A foot rub	☐ My prince to come
☐ The toothpaste capped	☐ A parking spot	☐ Chores completed	☐ A big bowl of ice cream
☐ A good hair day	☐ No tears	☐ Snuggle time	☐ A serenade
☐ Less laundry	☐ Stain-free day	☐ A good laugh	☐ Grace under pressure
☐ Window-shopping	☐ A haiku	☐ Clean sheets	☐ Mind over matter
☐ Complete obedience	☐ Cuddling	☐ A glass of bubbly	☐ Good will
☐ A chuckle	☐ Coddling	☐ Better neighbors	☐ Flowers
☐ Clean children	☐ A blowout	☐ To hear I'm cool	☐ A miracle
☐ A sincere compliment	☐ An empty dishwasher	☐ To hear I'm hot	☐ Some "me" time
☐ Mani-pedi	☐ You to put on a sweater	☐ Yoga	☐ A good cry
☐ A shoulder to cry on	☐ A nap	☐ Validation	☐ Girl's night out
☐ A random thoughtful act	☐ More help	☐ Breakfast in bed	☐ Romantic dinner
☐ To feel like a million bucks	☐ Complete silence	☐ Control of remote	☐ Full-time help
☐ To look like a million bucks	☐ Extra cheese	☐ A neck rub	☐ Just a little appreciation
☐ A million bucks	☐ A bra that fits	☐ A big smile	☐ Just you

☐ **PLEASE** ☐ **PRETTY PLEASE** ☐ **THANK YOU** ☐ **OR ELSE**

SIGNATURE (ACTUAL NAME OF MOTHER) | MONTH DAY YEAR

"IS IT REALLY SO MUCH TO ASK?"

THINGS MOM REALLY, REALLY, REALLY NEEDS

☐ **SOON**   ☐ **TODAY**   ☐ **RIGHT NOW**   ☐ **FROM NOW ON**

SOON	TODAY	RIGHT NOW	FROM NOW ON
☐ A break	☐ For you to read my mind	☐ Candlelight	☐ Movie night
☐ Less whine	☐ An aspirin	☐ Space	☐ A side of fries
☐ More wine	☐ Some respect	☐ A well-stocked fridge	☐ Some lovin'
☐ Your love	☐ Pizza, toppings my choice	☐ Commiseration	☐ A chauffeur
☐ Chocolate	☐ A good book	☐ To sleep in	☐ Inside voices
☐ A vacation	☐ Work-life balance	☐ A margarita	☐ A little more help
☐ Peace	☐ For you to make dinner	☐ Tantrum absence	☐ Vim
☐ Quiet	☐ A little enthusiasm	☐ The toilet seat down	☐ Vigor
☐ Peace and quiet	☐ To recapture my youth	☐ Someone to take out dog	☐ A good babysitter
☐ A date night	☐ Alone time	☐ Someone to bring in cat	☐ Soft lights
☐ The toilet paper replaced	☐ Alone time in bathroom	☐ A makeover	☐ Soft music
☐ Pampering	☐ Someone to admit I'm right	☐ Costume drama on DVR	☐ Clean clothes
☐ A kiss	☐ A shopping spree	☐ Reality TV on DVR	☐ Time to read
☐ A hug	☐ Attitude of gratitude	☐ Punctuality	☐ A day without dieting
☐ A bear hug	☐ Pie	☐ Endorphin rush	☐ Calm
☐ Someone to listen	☐ A massage	☐ Personal shopper	☐ A friendly phone call
☐ Takeout	☐ An ego massage	☐ Personal schlepper	☐ A day off
☐ A little help	☐ All the answers	☐ A mate to that sock	☐ A smidgen of kindness
☐ To fit into those jeans	☐ Any answer	☐ Time to reflect	☐ A good workout
☐ Privacy	☐ Sweet nothings	☐ A little consideration	☐ A new job
☐ A love note	☐ Personal trainer	☐ Spa day	☐ Even more wine
☐ No complaints	☐ Personal assistant	☐ To be fed grapes	☐ Utter devotion
☐ Hot coffee	☐ A cup of tea	☐ A stiff one	☐ Cupcakes
☐ A hot bath	☐ Therapy	☐ Mother's little helper	☐ Thermostat control
☐ A cold shower	☐ A good night's sleep	☐ A pep talk	☐ A cold drink
☐ Some good gossip	☐ Jewelry	☐ Fewer interruptions	☐ Inner peace
☐ A day in pajamas	☐ To be the center of attention	☐ To win	☐ A day without poop
☐ A day out of sweats	☐ To sit down for a minute	☐ A sugar fix	☐ Sympathy
☐ New shoes	☐ A happy child	☐ Well-behaved inner child	☐ Empathy
☐ A bit of effort	☐ A happy spouse	☐ Well-behaved children	☐ A comfy chair
☐ Barf-free clothing	☐ Praise for my intellect	☐ To get outside	☐ Second helping of dessert
☐ Stress relief	☐ Deodorant	☐ A guilty pleasure	☐ A brisk walk
☐ Family dinner	☐ An apology	☐ A primal scream	☐ A "Please"
☐ Beds all made	☐ Lottery win	☐ A clean kitchen	☐ A "Thank you"
☐ A pick-me-up	☐ A six-pack	☐ More chocolate	☐ A present
☐ Fireman fantasy	☐ Dust bunny eradication	☐ A foot rub	☐ My prince to come
☐ The toothpaste capped	☐ A parking spot	☐ Chores completed	☐ A big bowl of ice cream
☐ A good hair day	☐ No tears	☐ Snuggle time	☐ A serenade
☐ Less laundry	☐ Stain-free day	☐ A good laugh	☐ Grace under pressure
☐ Window-shopping	☐ A haiku	☐ Clean sheets	☐ Mind over matter
☐ Complete obedience	☐ Cuddling	☐ A glass of bubbly	☐ Good will
☐ A chuckle	☐ Coddling	☐ Better neighbors	☐ Flowers
☐ Clean children	☐ A blowout	☐ To hear I'm cool	☐ A miracle
☐ A sincere compliment	☐ An empty dishwasher	☐ To hear I'm hot	☐ Some "me" time
☐ Mani-pedi	☐ You to put on a sweater	☐ Yoga	☐ A good cry
☐ A shoulder to cry on	☐ A nap	☐ Validation	☐ Girl's night out
☐ A random thoughtful act	☐ More help	☐ Breakfast in bed	☐ Romantic dinner
☐ To feel like a million bucks	☐ Complete silence	☐ Control of remote	☐ Full-time help
☐ To look like a million bucks	☐ Extra cheese	☐ A neck rub	☐ Just a little appreciation
☐ A million bucks	☐ A bra that fits	☐ A big smile	☐ Just you

☐ **PLEASE**   ☐ **PRETTY PLEASE**   ☐ **THANK YOU**   ☐ **OR ELSE**

SIGNATURE (ACTUAL NAME OF MOTHER)

| MONTH | DAY | YEAR |

"IS IT REALLY SO MUCH TO ASK?"

THINGS MOM REALLY, REALLY, REALLY NEEDS

☐ **SOON**   ☐ **TODAY**   ☐ **RIGHT NOW**   ☐ **FROM NOW ON**

☐ A break	☐ For you to read my mind	☐ Candlelight	☐ Movie night
☐ Less whine	☐ An aspirin	☐ Space	☐ A side of fries
☐ More wine	☐ Some respect	☐ A well-stocked fridge	☐ Some lovin'
☐ Your love	☐ Pizza, toppings my choice	☐ Commiseration	☐ A chauffeur
☐ Chocolate	☐ A good book	☐ To sleep in	☐ Inside voices
☐ A vacation	☐ Work-life balance	☐ A margarita	☐ A little more help
☐ Peace	☐ For you to make dinner	☐ Tantrum absence	☐ Vim
☐ Quiet	☐ A little enthusiasm	☐ The toilet seat down	☐ Vigor
☐ Peace and quiet	☐ To recapture my youth	☐ Someone to take out dog	☐ A good babysitter
☐ A date night	☐ Alone time	☐ Someone to bring in cat	☐ Soft lights
☐ The toilet paper replaced	☐ Alone time in bathroom	☐ A makeover	☐ Soft music
☐ Pampering	☐ Someone to admit I'm right	☐ Costume drama on DVR	☐ Clean clothes
☐ A kiss	☐ A shopping spree	☐ Reality TV on DVR	☐ Time to read
☐ A hug	☐ Attitude of gratitude	☐ Punctuality	☐ A day without dieting
☐ A bear hug	☐ Pie	☐ Endorphin rush	☐ Calm
☐ Someone to listen	☐ A massage	☐ Personal shopper	☐ A friendly phone call
☐ Takeout	☐ An ego massage	☐ Personal schlepper	☐ A day off
☐ A little help	☐ All the answers	☐ A mate to that sock	☐ A smidgen of kindness
☐ To fit into those jeans	☐ Any answer	☐ Time to reflect	☐ A good workout
☐ Privacy	☐ Sweet nothings	☐ A little consideration	☐ A new job
☐ A love note	☐ Personal trainer	☐ Spa day	☐ Even more wine
☐ No complaints	☐ Personal assistant	☐ To be fed grapes	☐ Utter devotion
☐ Hot coffee	☐ A cup of tea	☐ A stiff one	☐ Cupcakes
☐ A hot bath	☐ Therapy	☐ Mother's little helper	☐ Thermostat control
☐ A cold shower	☐ A good night's sleep	☐ A pep talk	☐ A cold drink
☐ Some good gossip	☐ Jewelry	☐ Fewer interruptions	☐ Inner peace
☐ A day in pajamas	☐ To be the center of attention	☐ To win	☐ A day without poop
☐ A day out of sweats	☐ To sit down for a minute	☐ A sugar fix	☐ Sympathy
☐ New shoes	☐ A happy child	☐ Well-behaved inner child	☐ Empathy
☐ A bit of effort	☐ A happy spouse	☐ Well-behaved children	☐ A comfy chair
☐ Barf-free clothing	☐ Praise for my intellect	☐ To get outside	☐ Second helping of dessert
☐ Stress relief	☐ Deodorant	☐ A guilty pleasure	☐ A brisk walk
☐ Family dinner	☐ An apology	☐ A primal scream	☐ A "Please"
☐ Beds all made	☐ Lottery win	☐ A clean kitchen	☐ A "Thank you"
☐ A pick-me-up	☐ A six-pack	☐ More chocolate	☐ A present
☐ Fireman fantasy	☐ Dust bunny eradication	☐ A foot rub	☐ My prince to come
☐ The toothpaste capped	☐ A parking spot	☐ Chores completed	☐ A big bowl of ice cream
☐ A good hair day	☐ No tears	☐ Snuggle time	☐ A serenade
☐ Less laundry	☐ Stain-free day	☐ A good laugh	☐ Grace under pressure
☐ Window-shopping	☐ A haiku	☐ Clean sheets	☐ Mind over matter
☐ Complete obedience	☐ Cuddling	☐ A glass of bubbly	☐ Good will
☐ A chuckle	☐ Coddling	☐ Better neighbors	☐ Flowers
☐ Clean children	☐ A blowout	☐ To hear I'm cool	☐ A miracle
☐ A sincere compliment	☐ An empty dishwasher	☐ To hear I'm hot	☐ Some "me" time
☐ Mani-pedi	☐ You to put on a sweater	☐ Yoga	☐ A good cry
☐ A shoulder to cry on	☐ A nap	☐ Validation	☐ Girl's night out
☐ A random thoughtful act	☐ More help	☐ Breakfast in bed	☐ Romantic dinner
☐ To feel like a million bucks	☐ Complete silence	☐ Control of remote	☐ Full-time help
☐ To look like a million bucks	☐ Extra cheese	☐ A neck rub	☐ Just a little appreciation
☐ A million bucks	☐ A bra that fits	☐ A big smile	☐ Just you

☐ **PLEASE**   ☐ **PRETTY PLEASE**   ☐ **THANK YOU**   ☐ **OR ELSE**

SIGNATURE (ACTUAL NAME OF MOTHER)   MONTH   DAY   YEAR

"IS IT REALLY SO MUCH TO ASK?"

THINGS MOM REALLY, REALLY, REALLY NEEDS

☐ **SOON**   ☐ **TODAY**   ☐ **RIGHT NOW**   ☐ **FROM NOW ON**

SOON	TODAY	RIGHT NOW	FROM NOW ON
☐ A break	☐ For you to read my mind	☐ Candlelight	☐ Movie night
☐ Less whine	☐ An aspirin	☐ Space	☐ A side of fries
☐ More wine	☐ Some respect	☐ A well-stocked fridge	☐ Some lovin'
☐ Your love	☐ Pizza, toppings my choice	☐ Commiseration	☐ A chauffeur
☐ Chocolate	☐ A good book	☐ To sleep in	☐ Inside voices
☐ A vacation	☐ Work-life balance	☐ A margarita	☐ A little more help
☐ Peace	☐ For you to make dinner	☐ Tantrum absence	☐ Vim
☐ Quiet	☐ A little enthusiasm	☐ The toilet seat down	☐ Vigor
☐ Peace and quiet	☐ To recapture my youth	☐ Someone to take out dog	☐ A good babysitter
☐ A date night	☐ Alone time	☐ Someone to bring in cat	☐ Soft lights
☐ The toilet paper replaced	☐ Alone time in bathroom	☐ A makeover	☐ Soft music
☐ Pampering	☐ Someone to admit I'm right	☐ Costume drama on DVR	☐ Clean clothes
☐ A kiss	☐ A shopping spree	☐ Reality TV on DVR	☐ Time to read
☐ A hug	☐ Attitude of gratitude	☐ Punctuality	☐ A day without dieting
☐ A bear hug	☐ Pie	☐ Endorphin rush	☐ Calm
☐ Someone to listen	☐ A massage	☐ Personal shopper	☐ A friendly phone call
☐ Takeout	☐ An ego massage	☐ Personal schlepper	☐ A day off
☐ A little help	☐ All the answers	☐ A mate to that sock	☐ A smidgen of kindness
☐ To fit into those jeans	☐ Any answer	☐ Time to reflect	☐ A good workout
☐ Privacy	☐ Sweet nothings	☐ A little consideration	☐ A new job
☐ A love note	☐ Personal trainer	☐ Spa day	☐ Even more wine
☐ No complaints	☐ Personal assistant	☐ To be fed grapes	☐ Utter devotion
☐ Hot coffee	☐ A cup of tea	☐ A stiff one	☐ Cupcakes
☐ A hot bath	☐ Therapy	☐ Mother's little helper	☐ Thermostat control
☐ A cold shower	☐ A good night's sleep	☐ A pep talk	☐ A cold drink
☐ Some good gossip	☐ Jewelry	☐ Fewer interruptions	☐ Inner peace
☐ A day in pajamas	☐ To be the center of attention	☐ To win	☐ A day without poop
☐ A day out of sweats	☐ To sit down for a minute	☐ A sugar fix	☐ Sympathy
☐ New shoes	☐ A happy child	☐ Well-behaved inner child	☐ Empathy
☐ A bit of effort	☐ A happy spouse	☐ Well-behaved children	☐ A comfy chair
☐ Barf-free clothing	☐ Praise for my intellect	☐ To get outside	☐ Second helping of dessert
☐ Stress relief	☐ Deodorant	☐ A guilty pleasure	☐ A brisk walk
☐ Family dinner	☐ An apology	☐ A primal scream	☐ A "Please"
☐ Beds all made	☐ Lottery win	☐ A clean kitchen	☐ A "Thank you"
☐ A pick-me-up	☐ A six-pack	☐ More chocolate	☐ A present
☐ Fireman fantasy	☐ Dust bunny eradication	☐ A foot rub	☐ My prince to come
☐ The toothpaste capped	☐ A parking spot	☐ Chores completed	☐ A big bowl of ice cream
☐ A good hair day	☐ No tears	☐ Snuggle time	☐ A serenade
☐ Less laundry	☐ Stain-free day	☐ A good laugh	☐ Grace under pressure
☐ Window-shopping	☐ A haiku	☐ Clean sheets	☐ Mind over matter
☐ Complete obedience	☐ Cuddling	☐ A glass of bubbly	☐ Good will
☐ A chuckle	☐ Coddling	☐ Better neighbors	☐ Flowers
☐ Clean children	☐ A blowout	☐ To hear I'm cool	☐ A miracle
☐ A sincere compliment	☐ An empty dishwasher	☐ To hear I'm hot	☐ Some "me" time
☐ Mani-pedi	☐ You to put on a sweater	☐ Yoga	☐ A good cry
☐ A shoulder to cry on	☐ A nap	☐ Validation	☐ Girl's night out
☐ A random thoughtful act	☐ More help	☐ Breakfast in bed	☐ Romantic dinner
☐ To feel like a million bucks	☐ Complete silence	☐ Control of remote	☐ Full-time help
☐ To look like a million bucks	☐ Extra cheese	☐ A neck rub	☐ Just a little appreciation
☐ A million bucks	☐ A bra that fits	☐ A big smile	☐ Just you

☐ **PLEASE**   ☐ **PRETTY PLEASE**   ☐ **THANK YOU**   ☐ **OR ELSE**

SIGNATURE (ACTUAL NAME OF MOTHER)   MONTH : DAY : YEAR

"IS IT REALLY SO MUCH TO ASK?"

THINGS MOM REALLY, REALLY, REALLY NEEDS

☐ **SOON** ☐ **TODAY** ☐ **RIGHT NOW** ☐ **FROM NOW ON**

SOON	TODAY	RIGHT NOW	FROM NOW ON
☐ A break	☐ For you to read my mind	☐ Candlelight	☐ Movie night
☐ Less whine	☐ An aspirin	☐ Space	☐ A side of fries
☐ More wine	☐ Some respect	☐ A well-stocked fridge	☐ Some lovin'
☐ Your love	☐ Pizza, toppings my choice	☐ Commiseration	☐ A chauffeur
☐ Chocolate	☐ A good book	☐ To sleep in	☐ Inside voices
☐ A vacation	☐ Work-life balance	☐ A margarita	☐ A little more help
☐ Peace	☐ For you to make dinner	☐ Tantrum absence	☐ Vim
☐ Quiet	☐ A little enthusiasm	☐ The toilet seat down	☐ Vigor
☐ Peace and quiet	☐ To recapture my youth	☐ Someone to take out dog	☐ A good babysitter
☐ A date night	☐ Alone time	☐ Someone to bring in cat	☐ Soft lights
☐ The toilet paper replaced	☐ Alone time in bathroom	☐ A makeover	☐ Soft music
☐ Pampering	☐ Someone to admit I'm right	☐ Costume drama on DVR	☐ Clean clothes
☐ A kiss	☐ A shopping spree	☐ Reality TV on DVR	☐ Time to read
☐ A hug	☐ Attitude of gratitude	☐ Punctuality	☐ A day without dieting
☐ A bear hug	☐ Pie	☐ Endorphin rush	☐ Calm
☐ Someone to listen	☐ A massage	☐ Personal shopper	☐ A friendly phone call
☐ Takeout	☐ An ego massage	☐ Personal schlepper	☐ A day off
☐ A little help	☐ All the answers	☐ A mate to that sock	☐ A smidgen of kindness
☐ To fit into those jeans	☐ Any answer	☐ Time to reflect	☐ A good workout
☐ Privacy	☐ Sweet nothings	☐ A little consideration	☐ A new job
☐ A love note	☐ Personal trainer	☐ Spa day	☐ Even more wine
☐ No complaints	☐ Personal assistant	☐ To be fed grapes	☐ Utter devotion
☐ Hot coffee	☐ A cup of tea	☐ A stiff one	☐ Cupcakes
☐ A hot bath	☐ Therapy	☐ Mother's little helper	☐ Thermostat control
☐ A cold shower	☐ A good night's sleep	☐ A pep talk	☐ A cold drink
☐ Some good gossip	☐ Jewelry	☐ Fewer interruptions	☐ Inner peace
☐ A day in pajamas	☐ To be the center of attention	☐ To win	☐ A day without poop
☐ A day out of sweats	☐ To sit down for a minute	☐ A sugar fix	☐ Sympathy
☐ New shoes	☐ A happy child	☐ Well-behaved inner child	☐ Empathy
☐ A bit of effort	☐ A happy spouse	☐ Well-behaved children	☐ A comfy chair
☐ Barf-free clothing	☐ Praise for my intellect	☐ To get outside	☐ Second helping of dessert
☐ Stress relief	☐ Deodorant	☐ A guilty pleasure	☐ A brisk walk
☐ Family dinner	☐ An apology	☐ A primal scream	☐ A "Please"
☐ Beds all made	☐ Lottery win	☐ A clean kitchen	☐ A "Thank you"
☐ A pick-me-up	☐ A six-pack	☐ More chocolate	☐ A present
☐ Fireman fantasy	☐ Dust bunny eradication	☐ A foot rub	☐ My prince to come
☐ The toothpaste capped	☐ A parking spot	☐ Chores completed	☐ A big bowl of ice cream
☐ A good hair day	☐ No tears	☐ Snuggle time	☐ A serenade
☐ Less laundry	☐ Stain-free day	☐ A good laugh	☐ Grace under pressure
☐ Window-shopping	☐ A haiku	☐ Clean sheets	☐ Mind over matter
☐ Complete obedience	☐ Cuddling	☐ A glass of bubbly	☐ Good will
☐ A chuckle	☐ Coddling	☐ Better neighbors	☐ Flowers
☐ Clean children	☐ A blowout	☐ To hear I'm cool	☐ A miracle
☐ A sincere compliment	☐ An empty dishwasher	☐ To hear I'm hot	☐ Some "me" time
☐ Mani-pedi	☐ You to put on a sweater	☐ Yoga	☐ A good cry
☐ A shoulder to cry on	☐ A nap	☐ Validation	☐ Girl's night out
☐ A random thoughtful act	☐ More help	☐ Breakfast in bed	☐ Romantic dinner
☐ To feel like a million bucks	☐ Complete silence	☐ Control of remote	☐ Full-time help
☐ To look like a million bucks	☐ Extra cheese	☐ A neck rub	☐ Just a little appreciation
☐ A million bucks	☐ A bra that fits	☐ A big smile	☐ Just you

☐ **PLEASE** ☐ **PRETTY PLEASE** ☐ **THANK YOU** ☐ **OR ELSE**

SIGNATURE (ACTUAL NAME OF MOTHER) | MONTH DAY YEAR

"IS IT REALLY SO MUCH TO ASK?"

THINGS MOM REALLY, REALLY, REALLY NEEDS

☐ **SOON** ☐ **TODAY** ☐ **RIGHT NOW** ☐ **FROM NOW ON**

SOON	TODAY	RIGHT NOW	FROM NOW ON
☐ A break	☐ For you to read my mind	☐ Candlelight	☐ Movie night
☐ Less whine	☐ An aspirin	☐ Space	☐ A side of fries
☐ More wine	☐ Some respect	☐ A well-stocked fridge	☐ Some lovin'
☐ Your love	☐ Pizza, toppings my choice	☐ Commiseration	☐ A chauffeur
☐ Chocolate	☐ A good book	☐ To sleep in	☐ Inside voices
☐ A vacation	☐ Work-life balance	☐ A margarita	☐ A little more help
☐ Peace	☐ For you to make dinner	☐ Tantrum absence	☐ Vim
☐ Quiet	☐ A little enthusiasm	☐ The toilet seat down	☐ Vigor
☐ Peace and quiet	☐ To recapture my youth	☐ Someone to take out dog	☐ A good babysitter
☐ A date night	☐ Alone time	☐ Someone to bring in cat	☐ Soft lights
☐ The toilet paper replaced	☐ Alone time in bathroom	☐ A makeover	☐ Soft music
☐ Pampering	☐ Someone to admit I'm right	☐ Costume drama on DVR	☐ Clean clothes
☐ A kiss	☐ A shopping spree	☐ Reality TV on DVR	☐ Time to read
☐ A hug	☐ Attitude of gratitude	☐ Punctuality	☐ A day without dieting
☐ A bear hug	☐ Pie	☐ Endorphin rush	☐ Calm
☐ Someone to listen	☐ A massage	☐ Personal shopper	☐ A friendly phone call
☐ Takeout	☐ An ego massage	☐ Personal schlepper	☐ A day off
☐ A little help	☐ All the answers	☐ A mate to that sock	☐ A smidgen of kindness
☐ To fit into those jeans	☐ Any answer	☐ Time to reflect	☐ A good workout
☐ Privacy	☐ Sweet nothings	☐ A little consideration	☐ A new job
☐ A love note	☐ Personal trainer	☐ Spa day	☐ Even more wine
☐ No complaints	☐ Personal assistant	☐ To be fed grapes	☐ Utter devotion
☐ Hot coffee	☐ A cup of tea	☐ A stiff one	☐ Cupcakes
☐ A hot bath	☐ Therapy	☐ Mother's little helper	☐ Thermostat control
☐ A cold shower	☐ A good night's sleep	☐ A pep talk	☐ A cold drink
☐ Some good gossip	☐ Jewelry	☐ Fewer interruptions	☐ Inner peace
☐ A day in pajamas	☐ To be the center of attention	☐ To win	☐ A day without poop
☐ A day out of sweats	☐ To sit down for a minute	☐ A sugar fix	☐ Sympathy
☐ New shoes	☐ A happy child	☐ Well-behaved inner child	☐ Empathy
☐ A bit of effort	☐ A happy spouse	☐ Well-behaved children	☐ A comfy chair
☐ Barf-free clothing	☐ Praise for my intellect	☐ To get outside	☐ Second helping of dessert
☐ Stress relief	☐ Deodorant	☐ A guilty pleasure	☐ A brisk walk
☐ Family dinner	☐ An apology	☐ A primal scream	☐ A "Please"
☐ Beds all made	☐ Lottery win	☐ A clean kitchen	☐ A "Thank you"
☐ A pick-me-up	☐ A six-pack	☐ More chocolate	☐ A present
☐ Fireman fantasy	☐ Dust bunny eradication	☐ A foot rub	☐ My prince to come
☐ The toothpaste capped	☐ A parking spot	☐ Chores completed	☐ A big bowl of ice cream
☐ A good hair day	☐ No tears	☐ Snuggle time	☐ A serenade
☐ Less laundry	☐ Stain-free day	☐ A good laugh	☐ Grace under pressure
☐ Window-shopping	☐ A haiku	☐ Clean sheets	☐ Mind over matter
☐ Complete obedience	☐ Cuddling	☐ A glass of bubbly	☐ Good will
☐ A chuckle	☐ Coddling	☐ Better neighbors	☐ Flowers
☐ Clean children	☐ A blowout	☐ To hear I'm cool	☐ A miracle
☐ A sincere compliment	☐ An empty dishwasher	☐ To hear I'm hot	☐ Some "me" time
☐ Mani-pedi	☐ You to put on a sweater	☐ Yoga	☐ A good cry
☐ A shoulder to cry on	☐ A nap	☐ Validation	☐ Girl's night out
☐ A random thoughtful act	☐ More help	☐ Breakfast in bed	☐ Romantic dinner
☐ To feel like a million bucks	☐ Complete silence	☐ Control of remote	☐ Full-time help
☐ To look like a million bucks	☐ Extra cheese	☐ A neck rub	☐ Just a little appreciation
☐ A million bucks	☐ A bra that fits	☐ A big smile	☐ Just you

☐ **PLEASE**   ☐ **PRETTY PLEASE**   ☐ **THANK YOU**   ☐ **OR ELSE**

SIGNATURE (ACTUAL NAME OF MOTHER)

MONTH	DAY	YEAR

"IS IT REALLY SO MUCH TO ASK?"

KNOCKKNOCKSTUFF.COM ■ © 2014 WHO'S THERE INC.

THINGS MOM REALLY, REALLY, REALLY NEEDS

☐ **SOON**   ☐ **TODAY**   ☐ **RIGHT NOW**   ☐ **FROM NOW ON**

☐ A break	☐ For you to read my mind	☐ Candlelight	☐ Movie night
☐ Less whine	☐ An aspirin	☐ Space	☐ A side of fries
☐ More wine	☐ Some respect	☐ A well-stocked fridge	☐ Some lovin'
☐ Your love	☐ Pizza, toppings my choice	☐ Commiseration	☐ A chauffeur
☐ Chocolate	☐ A good book	☐ To sleep in	☐ Inside voices
☐ A vacation	☐ Work-life balance	☐ A margarita	☐ A little more help
☐ Peace	☐ For you to make dinner	☐ Tantrum absence	☐ Vim
☐ Quiet	☐ A little enthusiasm	☐ The toilet seat down	☐ Vigor
☐ Peace and quiet	☐ To recapture my youth	☐ Someone to take out dog	☐ A good babysitter
☐ A date night	☐ Alone time	☐ Someone to bring in cat	☐ Soft lights
☐ The toilet paper replaced	☐ Alone time in bathroom	☐ A makeover	☐ Soft music
☐ Pampering	☐ Someone to admit I'm right	☐ Costume drama on DVR	☐ Clean clothes
☐ A kiss	☐ A shopping spree	☐ Reality TV on DVR	☐ Time to read
☐ A hug	☐ Attitude of gratitude	☐ Punctuality	☐ A day without dieting
☐ A bear hug	☐ Pie	☐ Endorphin rush	☐ Calm
☐ Someone to listen	☐ A massage	☐ Personal shopper	☐ A friendly phone call
☐ Takeout	☐ An ego massage	☐ Personal schlepper	☐ A day off
☐ A little help	☐ All the answers	☐ A mate to that sock	☐ A smidgen of kindness
☐ To fit into those jeans	☐ Any answer	☐ Time to reflect	☐ A good workout
☐ Privacy	☐ Sweet nothings	☐ A little consideration	☐ A new job
☐ A love note	☐ Personal trainer	☐ Spa day	☐ Even more wine
☐ No complaints	☐ Personal assistant	☐ To be fed grapes	☐ Utter devotion
☐ Hot coffee	☐ A cup of tea	☐ A stiff one	☐ Cupcakes
☐ A hot bath	☐ Therapy	☐ Mother's little helper	☐ Thermostat control
☐ A cold shower	☐ A good night's sleep	☐ A pep talk	☐ A cold drink
☐ Some good gossip	☐ Jewelry	☐ Fewer interruptions	☐ Inner peace
☐ A day in pajamas	☐ To be the center of attention	☐ To win	☐ A day without poop
☐ A day out of sweats	☐ To sit down for a minute	☐ A sugar fix	☐ Sympathy
☐ New shoes	☐ A happy child	☐ Well-behaved inner child	☐ Empathy
☐ A bit of effort	☐ A happy spouse	☐ Well-behaved children	☐ A comfy chair
☐ Barf-free clothing	☐ Praise for my intellect	☐ To get outside	☐ Second helping of dessert
☐ Stress relief	☐ Deodorant	☐ A guilty pleasure	☐ A brisk walk
☐ Family dinner	☐ An apology	☐ A primal scream	☐ A "Please"
☐ Beds all made	☐ Lottery win	☐ A clean kitchen	☐ A "Thank you"
☐ A pick-me-up	☐ A six-pack	☐ More chocolate	☐ A present
☐ Fireman fantasy	☐ Dust bunny eradication	☐ A foot rub	☐ My prince to come
☐ The toothpaste capped	☐ A parking spot	☐ Chores completed	☐ A big bowl of ice cream
☐ A good hair day	☐ No tears	☐ Snuggle time	☐ A serenade
☐ Less laundry	☐ Stain-free day	☐ A good laugh	☐ Grace under pressure
☐ Window-shopping	☐ A haiku	☐ Clean sheets	☐ Mind over matter
☐ Complete obedience	☐ Cuddling	☐ A glass of bubbly	☐ Good will
☐ A chuckle	☐ Coddling	☐ Better neighbors	☐ Flowers
☐ Clean children	☐ A blowout	☐ To hear I'm cool	☐ A miracle
☐ A sincere compliment	☐ An empty dishwasher	☐ To hear I'm hot	☐ Some "me" time
☐ Mani-pedi	☐ You to put on a sweater	☐ Yoga	☐ A good cry
☐ A shoulder to cry on	☐ A nap	☐ Validation	☐ Girl's night out
☐ A random thoughtful act	☐ More help	☐ Breakfast in bed	☐ Romantic dinner
☐ To feel like a million bucks	☐ Complete silence	☐ Control of remote	☐ Full-time help
☐ To look like a million bucks	☐ Extra cheese	☐ A neck rub	☐ Just a little appreciation
☐ A million bucks	☐ A bra that fits	☐ A big smile	☐ Just you

☐ **PLEASE**   ☐ **PRETTY PLEASE**   ☐ **THANK YOU**   ☐ **OR ELSE**

SIGNATURE (ACTUAL NAME OF MOTHER)   MONTH : DAY : YEAR

"IS IT REALLY SO MUCH TO ASK?"